Mature Christianity

*For come-of-age Christians
in a come-of-age world*

by
William A. Holmes

resurgence publishing corporation

www.ResurgencePublishing.com

Info@ResurgencePublishing.com

www.ResurgencePublishing.com

Cover graphics image attributed to Wordle™ at http://www.wordle.net

Cover design by Richard G. Walters, 2010

Printed on recycled paper

ISBN 0-9763892-3-1

Printed in the United States of America

TO OUR SONS WILL AND CHRIS

who model in their maturity

what this book is about

Preface

In the middle of the 19th Century, the Danish theologian, Soren Kierkegaard, told the grim parable about a fire that breaks out backstage just before a circus is to perform. In panic, the stage manager sends out a clown, already in costume, to warn the audience. But the spectators take his desperate pleas as part of an act, and the more he gesticulates, the more they laugh, until fire engulfs the entire theater.

Kierkegaard suggests we Christians are in a similar situation: The more we gesticulate with our funny creeds and doctrines, the more laughable we seem to a skeptical world. If only we changed out of our ridiculous costumes, he implies, there would be a far greater likelihood that we would be taken seriously. Kierkegaard does not exactly say which creedal formulas we should strip off, nor what new theological apparel he would have us put on to make ourselves more credible. But, if his own writings provide us with a clue, what we have to say about God better be a radical departure from previous habits.

This book is an attempt at such a departure. This is not to say that I take the Christian faith to be merely a disposable wrap which can be exchanged for the latest fashion. On the contrary, as Kierkegaard would himself insist, there is an objective integrity to the Gospel which must be conveyed from one generation to the next. But since there is no such thing as an "un-interpreted" experience, and since all accounts of God are subjective accounts of someone's experience, it stands to reason that interpretations of experiences will vary and different "orthodoxies" will appear and eventually disappear. The Word of God revealed in Jesus Christ will always come to us in what the New Testament calls "earthen vessels." With the intent of abiding by "the faith which was once for all delivered to the saints", [1] I have endeavored in these pages to put on the garb of a new millennium, and to speak to a generation of Christians come-of-age in a world come-of-age – even though I have no doubt there will be persons who will think I've dressed for fashion at the expense of the Gospel, while others will find my new attire even more ridiculous than the funny costume it replaced.

Nevertheless, I am convinced that an ecclesiastical version of James Baldwin's *The Fire Next Time* is here. The fires of social, political and economic crises threaten to leave only the charred remains of a once relevant institution, and there must be those of us "on the inside" willing to sound the alarm and point to alternative, life-saving exits. Our priority is not the survival of the institution per se (the theater or the church), but acting out a drama which reclaims the world for the humanizing, civilizing process. The church, like the theater, exists only to rehearse and actualize that drama for the sake of renewing the world.

The audience for whom I've written is not the average Christian. Polls in the early part of this new century showed that eight in ten Americans insist that they never doubt the existence of God, and eighty-two percent told the Gallup International Millennium Survey that God is "very important to them." (2) My hunch is that the vast majority of these persons is assiduously content in their religion and would consider this little book a false alarm.

At the same time, there are significant numbers of women and men for whom God's existence and significance are problematic, and for whom the God hypothesis no longer works. A surprising number of these persons are still in our churches, while others have left or are on their way out. In April of 2009, the Pew Forum on Religion & Public Life published the results of a large-scale study indicating: Almost three-quarters of Roman Catholics and Protestants now unaffiliated with a religion say they "just gradually drifted away" from their faith. And more than three-quarters of Catholics and half of Protestants currently unrelated to a church said that over time, they stopped believing in their religion's teachings. Unlike the popular perception that most of these persons have embraced secularism, a number remain surprisingly open to religious perspectives, and according to researchers, say that they have just not yet found the right religion. (3) To the extent that these persons are living in a world come-of-age, it is to this constituency that I hope to speak with some credibility, as well as to those clergy who believe, as I do, that it is still possible to proclaim the Christian faith in a compelling way without insulting the modern mind. (4)

I write as a pastor and preacher with extraordinary access to people's lives. With the possible exception of physicians, I know of no one with more opportunities than clergy to share in sentinel events that create and transform the human journey: birth and death, marriage and separation, joys and sorrows – those times in life when old continuities disappear and new possibilities come into being. In addition, for 24 years at my denomination's National Church in Washington, D.C., I have mounted the pulpit and labored to proclaim a message that was faithful to my ordination while also being creative and intellectually honest. I hope this literary effort will be seen as consistent with, and a continuation of, that effort.

Although not an academician, my clerical world is continuously nourished, challenged and enriched by the scholarship of others. I am particularly indebted to the writings of Karen Armstrong, Marcus J. Borg, John Dominic Crossan, Robert W. Funk, and John Shelby Spong, along with other scholars in the Jesus Seminar school. I see myself as a kind of "theological midwife" whose task is to help people give birth to reflections about the experience of being human, and to discover how the Word in Jesus Christ illumines and interprets that experience. I am convinced that lay persons seriously raising the great questions of life, can profit immeasurably from the insights of Christian scholars and theologians.

While much of what appears in the early chapters of this book reflects my indebtedness to certain contemporary biblical and theological scholars, I have intentionally devoted some of the later chapters to selected passages from Soren Kierkegaard, and to two prominent theologians of the 20th century: Dietrich Bonhoeffer and Paul Tillich. I find Kierkegaard's metaphors and parables as powerful today as they were over 160 years ago, and the names of Bonhoeffer and Tillich – and in many instances their writings – are familiar to a large number of informed laity and clergy. I believe that the theological insights of these two men, more than any others of the previous century, anticipated the present crises in the church's loss of credibility, and laid a foundation for envisioning the Christian life in ways both radical and faithful in this new millennium.

I have attempted to put many of their insights into my own words, with documentation, because they are so germane to my opening thesis, and because I want to assure my reader that this book is not inventing but expanding on theological concepts that have gone before us. I should add that even though I am not a professional scholar or expert in the theology of either Bonhoeffer or Tillich, I have read extensively in their writings; and I had the privilege of doing post-graduate studies at Union Theological Seminary in New York with Paul Tillich.

Initially I wondered about the length of what I've written, since most books are of some greater length than this one. But then I recalled that passage from Bonhoeffer's *Letters and Papers from Prison* where he introduces a basic outline of thoughts – later to be expanded on – by saying: "I should like to write a book of not more than 100 pages, divided into three chapters." (5) Although I can't presume a comparison to his writings, and even though my chapters are more than the number he projected, I take courage from Bonhoeffer's example of a shorter work offered without apology. Also, I'm hoping that this little book will be received like a brief homily: If it is well received, my audience may wish that it was longer; if it disappoints, the reader will be glad it ended sooner rather than later.

After completing the initial draft of this manuscript, I reviewed from the beginning what I had written. It was then, for the first time, I discovered a pattern in at least a majority of the chapters. That pattern reminded me of another Soren Kierkegaard story about a man who writes a novel in which one of the characters goes mad. While working on the book, the author himself gradually goes mad, and finishes it in the first person.

To the extent that the Christian faith is a special kind of "madness" that has afflicted both my personal and professional life, I discovered that in endeavoring to write about it, I have occasionally lapsed into accounts of personal experiences and illustrations. Like Kierkegaard's mad author, by the end of the book, I too finish in the first person. Whether this is an asset or a liability, I'm not altogether sure. I simply offer it as an observation.

In taking full responsibility for what appears here, I am also deeply indebted to several people whose suggestions and support have undergirded me along the way.

First and foremost has been my wife, Nancy, who patiently indulged me as I sat for hours before my computer, incommunicado, working on a project from which she was necessarily excluded. As the first person to see the initial draft of the manuscript, her insights and encouragement were critical to the projects content and to its author. It was Nancy who reminded me that the project itself would never have found its way to these pages without the counsel and support of our computer-expert and favorite (only) grandson, Taylor William Holmes. He has been our invaluable "tech" all along the way.

I am also grateful to my colleague and friend, R. Bruce Poynter. His many hours of reading and reflecting on what I've written made it possible for me to undertake a number of major revisions, as well as scores of editorial corrections. Similarly with the late Jolyon J. Johnston, Professor of Philosophy at Georgia Tech, a close friend since boyhood, he was a "closet theologian" if I ever saw one. Two colleagues in the active ministry, James M. Hunt, Sr., and my son, Christopher T. Holmes, offered helpful suggestions born of present-day experiences; and J. Philip Wogaman, a long-time friend, fellow minister, and formerly Professor of Chris-Christian Ethics at Wesley Theological Seminary in Washington, D.C., contributed a number of helpful insights. The late Ira G. Zepp, Jr., Professor Emeritus of Religious Studies at McDaniel College also reviewed the manuscript and offered the kind of encouragement and support that only he could give.

As former publishers, now retired, Jim and Betty Ann Angel reviewed a later draft of my manuscript; and Cynthia B. Stevens, M.D., P.C., in private practice as a psychiatrist and psychoanalyst while also serving on the faculty of the George Washington Medical School, graciously agreed to view what I have written through the lens of her own profession. No author ever had a publisher more supportive than Resurgence Publishing, and M. George Walters, along with John Epps, my editor, have offered the kind of guidance that has made the entire process a positive experience. They have recognized, as will most who read these pages, my profound indebtedness to the former Ecumenical Institute and to the late, Joseph Wesley Mathews

In conclusion, I must add that I have been much influenced by meeting regularly with an ecumenical group of colleagues which include clergy as well as college and seminary professors. Our purpose has been to stay as current as possible with the "cutting edge" of today's theology and biblical studies. Without listing their names, I offer these words of gratitude for their influence in my life, and register the hope that this literary effort will accurately reflect some of our more provocative struggles and reflections. In a word, this book was born in debt.

Note: All scripture references, unless otherwise noted, are from the New Revised Standard Version.

Notes and References

1. Jude 3

2. Washington Post, January 4, 20004, "Religion, the Eternal Growth Industry"

3. Ibid., April 28, 2009, "Study Examines Choice of Religion"

4. I am using "modern" in the sense of "contemporary." The expression in academia might well appear as "post-modern." In either instance, I am referring to persons who live in a world where scientific knowledge has replaced supernatural interventions.

5. The Macmillan Company, New York, 1968, p. 200

Introduction

The seeds of motivation for this book were sown a number of years ago when I first read a little work by Sigmund Freud entitled *The Future of an Illusion*. His thesis as to what constitutes an "illusion" created in me such a crisis of faith, that I've been reflecting on that crises and its provocations ever since. This book is a result of those reflections.

In summary, Freud's contention was as follows:

Let us imagine to ourselves the mental life of the small child . . . The libido follows the paths of narcissistic needs, and attaches itself to the objects that ensure their satisfaction. So the mother, who satisfies hunger, becomes the first love-object, and certainly also the first protection against all the undefined and threatening dangers of the outer world; becomes, if we may so express it, the first protection against anxiety.

In this function the mother is soon replaced by the stronger father, and this situation persists from now on over the whole of childhood. But the relation to the father is affected by a peculiar ambivalence. He was himself a danger, perhaps just because of that earlier relation to the mother; so he is feared no less than he is longed for and admired . . . Now when the child grows up and finds that he is destined to remain a child for ever, and that he can never do without protection against unknown and mighty powers, he invests these with the traits of the father-figure; he creates for himself the gods, of whom he is afraid, whom he seeks to propitiate, and whom he nevertheless entrusts the task of protecting him. [1]

As a young minister just finishing postgraduate studies, and reading the above contention for the first time, I found myself transfixed by the audacious possibility that there could be even the slightest credibility to Freud's analysis of why human beings are religious. His claim that the formation of religion and the development of the idea of God could be explained as a "longing-for-the father," and then to allege later in the book that "religion is comparable to a childhood neurosis" – all of that struck me as a radically serious indictment I had, until then, never considered.

College courses in psychology and seminary classes in pastoral counseling had introduced me to Freud's writings, and I was familiar with the Oedipus complex as an explanation of a subconscious sexual desire in a child, especially a male child, for the parent of the opposite sex. But the application of "Oedipus" as a way of accounting for the human dependency on God was, for me, a new and unsettling discovery. Since then, I have learned that many of Freud's theories, including "Oedipus," have been revised. (2) However, in my judgment, what defies revision and continues as one of Freud's most reliable insights is his analysis of that persistent longing of the child in each of us to be watched over, protected and rewarded.

To be sure, the early years of life are so vulnerable, so unprotected, that parental guardianship is imperative for basic survival. The world is a dangerous place for children, and from infancy forward we are dependent on parents for shelter, safety and other necessities for our well-being. But eventually, in various increments, we discover how much our parents are like us – fallible and finite. Gradually or suddenly we come to understand that they can't hold back the darkness, drive away evil, or eliminate danger. They don't have infinite knowledge, they often make mistakes, and on occasions they are overwhelmed and helpless. They even get sick and die. And since the world is still a dangerous and scary place, eventually we look beyond our parents for other guarantors of our well-being. It is at this point that, according to Freud, those of us who are religiously inclined, project our longing for security to a cosmic level and call it "God."

Throughout my ministry as an ordained minister in the United

Methodist Church, this disturbing part of Freud's analysis has reverbe-rated in the echo chamber of my consciousness, challenging both my personal faith and the integrity of my vocation. More than any other sin-gle proposition, it has driven me to think as radically as possible about God, and to devote my ministry to challenging congregations to grow beyond what the Apostle Paul called "childish ways." (3)

Initially I considered entitling these pages *"Christianity for Adults Only."* Even though the book contains absolutely nothing salacious (lead-ing perhaps to the disappointment of some prospective readers), friends eventually convinced me that I should choose a title less ambivalent – thus the more prudent, *Mature Christianity*. Never-the-less, I cling stub-bornly to my initial inclination, and hereby claim my author's prerogative to at least insist in this "Introduction" that what the book attempts to ex-plicate is, in fact, *"Christianity for Adults Only."*

I have written out of the conviction that no one reaches adulthood without experiencing the vulnerability of finitude, and that each of us re-sponds to that vulnerability by being either in denial of it, or by theologically reflecting on its implications. In one way or another, we ex-perience loss of meaning, pangs of guilt, the unpredictability of the future, the certainty of death, and, at least, on occasions, periods of des-pair. These existential levels of our humanity are the very levels to which the Gospel is addressed and to which this book is directed.

Furthermore, I am writing for adults living in a world of science and modernity, as opposed to a world of superstition and anachronisms. It is a world having much in common with the "flat world" described by Thomas L. Friedman in his best-selling book, *The World is Flat* (2005). On-ly, where Friedman argues that the convergence of technology and the global supply chain is "flattening" the earth, my thesis is that, "flat" or not, the earth is "disconnected." Theologically, it has slipped its superna-tural moorings and is no longer tied to a deity defined as hovering over us, directly accessible, and interceding on our behalf in times of crisis.

The "disconnect," however, is God's gift to us – the consequence of a holy love envisioning nothing less for creation than full maturity and independence.

To provide my reader with something of a "road map" as to what lies ahead: Chapter I is about the metaphor, "Father," as applied to God, its distortion, and how the metaphor is used in Old and New Testaments references. Chapter II considers the metaphor as it passes through various stages of human development, including when it's carried to its logical conclusion. Chapter III is about Dietrich Bonhoeffer's contention, as early as 1945, that humankind is already in a world where the God hypothesis is no longer needed – and yet, in such a world, what it means to live "without God, before God, with God." The fourth and fifth chapters explore Bonhoeffer's "ethics" and how, without divine guidance, come-of-age Christians can still know and do the will of God.

As a student of Paul Tillich, I have long believed that the Christian faith, seriously embraced, is consistent with what most professionals in psychology consider sound mental health. [4] Therefore, Chapters VI and VII consider how Tillich's theology explicitly addresses psychological issues. One of the chapters discusses his thoughts on the existential anxiety of every human being, while the second examines his concept of courage and what it means to live faithfully before the "God above God." And, finally, to the extent that this book represents an interpretation of the Christian faith *not* in ascendancy today, we consider in Chapter VIII what the spread of conservative, fundamentalist Christianity means for tomorrow's Christendom, and what that future holds for dwindling numbers of progressive Christians.

Throughout it all, the purpose of each chapter is to offer as strong a case as I can make for an interpretation of Christianity which seeks to leave "childish ways" behind. The opening sentence to John Calvin's *Institutes of Christian Religion* reads, "True and substantial wisdom consists principally of two parts: the knowledge of God and knowledge of ourselves." With the assumption that these two parts are inextricably joined, I invite the reader to accompany me on a venture combining theological reflection and revelatory insights from modern psychology. And, I hasten to add, my expectation of the reader is not that you necessarily agree with what I've written. Rather, I simply ask that you reflect with me along the way, applying the integrity of your own life-experiences to the subject of each chapter, and thereby determining whether a *Mature Christianity* illumines that life-experience or not.

Notes and References:

1. A Doubleday Anchor Book, Garden City, N.Y., 1957, p. p. 39-40

2. Freud considered the Oedipus complex to be his greatest discovery, and many   of his theories continue to have credibility within the practices of psychoanalysis, psychodynamic psychotherapy, and psychiatry in general.   However, the professional periodical, *Psychiatric News,* reports that, as far as the Oedipus complex is concerned, "Today psychiatrists tend to disagree with this assessment. Moreover, they are apt to question the universality of the concept." This challenging of "Oedipus" as a psycho/sexual concept does not, however, negate its relevancy as a "psycho/theological" concept. August 18, 2006, p. 9

3. For a more comprehensive analysis of stages of faith development, I would highly recommend the work that has been done over the past quarter century or so by James W. Fowler of Emory University. His <u>Faith Development Theory</u> is not only based on the developmental psychology of Jean Piaget and Erik Erikson, but also draws heavily on the work of the Harvard psychologist, Lawrence Kohlberg, and his model of moral development. While my definition of "maturity" in this book emphasizes self-reliance over dependency, and a theological model of God as incarnate in the sanctity of human life, I in no way intend for these accents to be seen as alternatives to Fowler's final stage of faith. On the contrary, I see them as complimentary to what he calls a "Universalizing Faith." Persons of such faith are devoted to overcoming division, oppression, and violence and live in anticipatory response to the eventual triumph of love and justice, the reality of the kingdom of God breaking – even now – upon our world.

4. The Latin *Salvus* (from which we get salve and salvation) originally had to do with healing. Hale, whole and health are interrelated. "Are you saved?" translates "Are you well, whole, healthy?"

Contents

Preface..v

Introduction 13

Chapter I: Faith, Fear and Fatherhood 21

Rethinking and Reclaiming the "Father" Metaphor for God 21

Chapter II: When Christians Come of Age...................................33

Carrying the "Father" Metaphor to Its Logical Conclusion............33

Chapter III: Bonhoeffer on "Religionless Christianity" 41

Living without God, before God, with God....................................41

Chapter IV: Bonhoeffer's Ethics 53

Making Ethical Decisions without "Divine Guidance" 53

Chapter V: Cold Facts about Hot Issues 69

How our lust for certitude divides the world................................69

Chapter VI: Redefining "Mental Health" 87

Embracing Vulnerability and Existential Anxiety..........................87

Chapter VII: Courage and the "God above God" 101

Living as a 21st Century Person of Faith 101

Chapter VIII: Tomorrow's Christendom 115

The Future of Post-Theistic Christianity.....................................115

Conclusion 137

About the Author...143

Chapter I: Faith, Fear and Fatherhood

Rethinking and Reclaiming the "Father" Metaphor for God

For 46 years of ministry, I have been impressed with how meaningful the "Father" metaphor for God has been to the large majority of my parishioners. It is, by far the most popular expression for a transcendent being. This is not withstanding the fact that in the last century, the traditionally masculine features of fatherhood were enriched to include tenderness and nurturing – features which, although not limited exclusively to women, made it possible for some to speak of God as "Mother." And, of course, for centuries, the sainthood of The Virgin Mary provided Roman Catholics with a connection to the maternal. However, irrespective of these developments, and regardless of the fact that both Old and New Testaments contain other analogies, metaphors and synonyms for God, the paternal metaphor has remained the preeminent image out of which most Christians conceive of themselves as "children of a Heavenly Father."

While all the above is true, over the same period of time, I have also observed a gradual *decline* in the power and influence of the "Father" metaphor. A growing number of persons in congregations have stopped thinking of themselves as "children" under the protective guidance of a "super parent," and have begun wondering whether this departure disqualifies them from participation in the Christian community. Even though the "Father" metaphor has long endured in the church's lexicon of references to God, modern questions continue to be raised about its meaning in a post- Copernican, post-Darwinian, post-Einsteinium world. And, as these questions are rebuffed or ignored within the church, many of the persons raising them have joined the exodus streaming out of mainline denominations.

I want to keep the questions and the persons raising them, *within* the institutional church. While, historically, the Christian faith predates and does not depend on laws of modern science or basic insights of modern psychology, there is good reason to believe it is not inimical to them either. Nothing about the Gospel requires the Church to be a refuge for pre-scientific concepts. Also, as we shall see, the idea of God as hovering over us like an anxious parent waiting to intervene, is not only an idea that deserves to be rethought, it is a gross distortion of genuine fatherhood, human and divine.

The case I want to make cannot be creditable without first "giving Sigmund Freud his due." He was on to something with his analysis of certain religious persons as insecure and needy, projecting a higher power to rescue them in times of peril. In a word, *fear* has always been the motivation for such dependency, and that fear is found as readily in contemporary religions – including much of Christianity – as in the animism of primitive societies. While a sense of awe and gratitude have also contributed to religious impulses, it is fear that has been, and continues to be in many instances, the prevailing motivation.

A Bit of History

Anthropologists have found that ancient religions give evidence of having been conceived in dread and apprehension. Primitive people experienced their existence as replete with threatening mysteries and hazardous conditions. They had no concept of what we call "natural death" or living long enough to reach "old age." Mostly, death came to them as a traumatic interruption of the life cycle through violence or disease. Confounded by droughts, floods and other weather changes, they also had to be on guard against the attacks of wild animals and often the hostility of other human beings. Through it all, they sought the favor of "gods" to intercede for them, believing with a fearful reverence that such deities could be influenced and appeased.

Objects of worship were everywhere. One of the first was probably the moon, which controlled the weather. The sun replaced the moon about the time that growing crops replaced hunting, and societies began ordering their lives around planting and reaping. Stars and constellations were worshiped, and the sky itself became a great god as the giver of rain. The earth too was deified, and the veneration of trees, springs, rivers and mountains is one of the oldest traceable religions. Primitive people trembled before the awfulness and awesomeness of their environment. Fear, as Lucretius said, was the mother of the gods.

Ancestor worship originated as a propitiation of the dead. It flourished in Egypt, Greece and Rome, and various forms of it survive today in China, Japan and more than a few countries in the Southern hemispheres. Initially, people were fearful that the dead would curse and blight their lives, but later, ancestor worship aroused the sentiment of awe, and finally developed piety and devotion. In fact, in *The Story of Civilization*, Will Durant observes, "It is the tendency of gods to begin as ogres and to end as loving fathers; the idol passes into an ideal as the growing security, peacefulness and moral sense of the worshipers pacify and transform the features of their once ferocious deities." [1]

For a number of years I have been a student and collector of masks from different societies and cultures. Two of the masks I most prize in my collection are from the Oaxaca region of Southern Mexico. The indigenous people of that area, Zapotec and Mixtec Indians, carved masks in the likenesses of animals and birds to replicate totems used to ward off evil spirits. As soon as a child was born, it was placed in the center of the village overnight. The next morning, elders checked for tracks. Whatever tracks came closest to the child during the night represented the animal or bird which became the child's guardian and sacred totem. Creatures of the wild were imbued with special powers.

With few exceptions, the reliance of primitive people upon gods to protect them is not unlike the reliance of children on their parents. The earliest of religions were cradled in dependency, propitiation and fear.

Fears That Still Beset Us

Even though we have outgrown a host of age-old superstitions and have expanded greatly on the myopic world-view once held by primitive peoples, for all our knowledge and sophistication, the primal fears of the human psyche remain. Those fears are as prevalent and existentially intense in us as they were in previous generations. Every one of us lives with a bone-deep sense of the precariousness of our existence, a vague awareness of the nuances and delicate balances by which we survive each day, and the inescapable reminders of contingencies and vulnerabilities which keep defining us as finite creatures.

TV newscasts compete to report the latest, scariest events; manufacturers make huge profits selling "safety products," and warning labels are so ubiquitous, they now appear on tubes of toothpaste. Most of us were on "orange alert" long before September 11, 2001. Even though the aim of terror is *terror,* the horrific moments of 9-11 didn't create something new in us; they magnified something already nascent.

Even in denial, we harbor a profound disquietude and dread of – what? Often, it's hard to name. At times, the dread gets localized in a diagnosis of cancer, or in the ravages conferred by a stroke, or heart disease, or AIDS, or Alzheimer's disease. It can take the form of a near-fatal automobile accident, or a violent crime, or a freighting force of nature – as in a tsunami, a hurricane or an earthquake. The death of a close friend or loved one can make the awareness of our own vulnerability so real that – whatever name we give it – we cannot escape the sense that "something lies in wait for us." Beyond all precautions, we live with a foreboding that at any moment, random and capricious forces can interrupt or end existence as we know it.

There is, of course, an important distinction to be made between fear and anxiety. Fear always has an object, and can be conquered by action. Anxiety, which we will discuss in greater depth in another chapter, has no specific object, and cannot be conquered. It is always present, although often it is latent, and it can exist along side of fear, as well as in situations where there is nothing to be feared.

The terrorists' attack of 9-11, and the Bush administration's reaction to it, more than any other event in recent history, not only unveiled America's deepest fears, it also revealed how easily our anxieties can be exploited. On the one hand, the shock of seeing the World Trade Center's Twin Towers ablaze, collapsing and interring several thousands of our fellow citizens produced what might well be called a logical fear of an enemy sworn to strike again. And, with few exceptions, countries throughout the world empathized with both our loss and our fear of further attacks. The headline of one foreign newspaper read "Today, We are All Americans." Consequently, the decision of the United States to declare war against the Taliban – al Qaeda's host in Afghanistan – was widely supported at the time by both the American people and the international community. It was understood as fear's logical response to a threat which could only be ignored at a greater peril.

At the same time, in addition to fear, anxiety was at work in the 9-11 equation – an anxiety which had no specific object but manifest itself as a profound unease toward something shadowy and vague, unpredictable and unforeseen. We had no way of knowing whether other threatening powers "out there" might also be poised to do us harm. Seizing on this uncertainty, the Bush administration assured us that just such a threat *was* posed by Iraq; it not only harbored the instigators of 9-11, the proof of its sinister intent was in its "weapons of mass destruction." That "proof" became the pretext for a preemptive war, and, with the invasion underway, "the danger of changing the Commander and Chief in midstream" became the rallying point for Bush's narrow win of a presidential second term.

For Iraq, the U.S. invasion meant the death of approximately a million of its citizens, the widespread destruction of its infrastructure, and al Qaeda's exploitation of the country's devastation as a magnate for recruiting and training terrorists. For America, in addition to its own dead and wounded, the invasion meant curtailments of heretofore unassailable democratic freedoms in the name of "Homeland Security," the indenturing of future generations with massive fiscal burdens, the Attorney General's caricature of the Geneva Conventions as "quaint," and multiple explanations for the invasion of Iraq – each explanation, according to public opinion polls, less convincing than the others. Through exploitation of America's anxieties about the unknown and the unforeseen, the Bush administration led the nation into a quicksand of ever deepening tragedies and futile efforts. And now, with the Obama administration locating the primary efforts of the Taliban in Afghanistan and Pakistan (and at this writing, Yemen has been added), it remains to be seen how successful a major military offense can be in a land long known as "the burial ground of empires."

So, the world continues to be a scary place, and even though the psyches of modern men and women confront different forms of terror, our anxieties and fears are not all that different from those of ancient forebears. Like all who have gone before us, we long to be made safe from danger. And, perhaps for this same reason, our longing to be protected has caused us to presume that the "Father" metaphor for God is ultimately about "divine protection." However, this presumption is the projection of a security we long for, rather than an accurate depiction of the way the metaphor in most instances is biblically construed.

Biblical References to "Father"

Foreshadowed in the Old Testament and extended to early Judaism, the Jews believed that God had chosen them to be his people, and in this sense he had become their Father. The Hebrew term for "father" is reflected in the names of Abraham, Abimelech, Absalom and other patriarchs; and the idea of divine fatherhood is used with increasing frequency in Isaiah, Malachi, and other instances in the Jewish vocabulary of worship. In some Old Testament accounts, God is depicted as championing the Jews and granting them victory over their enemies. But in other instances, if not far more often, Jewish defeats and exiles are prophetically interpreted as God's judgment on a wayward people. It was Jesus who gave a new depth to the concept of God as "Father," exhibiting through his own life an attitude of sonship. The confirmation of that attitude was made explicit in his baptism at the hands of John the Baptist, with the voice from heaven saying, "You are my Son, the Beloved; with you I am well pleased." (Mark 1:11)

While Jesus used the designation for God as "Father" rather sparingly; it does appear in all the gospels, and most especially in Matthew and John. According to *The Interpreters Dictionary of the Bible*, "... there is no need to doubt that it is a genuine word of Jesus, and, representing a form of address to human fathers, it reflects in Jesus an unprecedented simplicity and directness of approach to God." [2] Also, New Testament scholars generally agree that Jesus undoubtedly employed the term "Abba" (Aramaic for "Father") to address God in the salutation of The Lord's Prayer, as well as on other occasions. The approbation even carried over to the doctrine of the Trinity. Although nowhere in the New Testament is that doctrine made explicit, most scholars believe the seeds of a Trinitarian understanding of God are sewn, and that there is strong Biblical support for the first person of the trinity as "Father." [3]

However, the central question of this chapter is not: "Did Jesus refer to God as 'Father'"? (Quite clearly, he did.) The issue to be examined here is whether Jesus intended for the "Father" metaphor primarily to convey an image of God as *protector*, or did he have some other parental emphasis in mind? What was his intent when he invited us to pray "Our Father"?

Biblical "Maturity"

This chapter is grounded in the conviction that the Bible has the maturity theme running through it like a deep, underground stream which surfaces at times to become explicit. Not that it is the only stream, and not that there aren't other streams that flow in different directions. But on the whole, given the cumulative integrity of the biblical message, the theme of living a caring, self-reliant existence before God is more consistent with the Bible's witness than any other.

In the traditional language of "salvation," what Christ saves us *from* is the self-deception that there is a "way out" of experiencing our lives as adults. It is a salvation *from* the wish-projection that God will provide alternatives to the real world, and *from* the pretension that being "religious" means being excused from having to make tough choices. Rather than offering a "way *out*" of having to live a mature life, Christ offers a "way *in*." He is "the way, the truth, and the life" because he lived his own life to the fullest while facing doubt, uncertainty and death – head-on. Courageously trusting God in the absence of any guarantees or proofs, he loved unconditionally and offered others the supreme example of what it means to be authentically human. As our "elder brother," he personified maturity *par excellence*.

In Matthew 5:48, the author of the Gospel quotes Jesus as saying, "Be perfect, therefore, as your heavenly Father is perfect." Kathleen Norris has an interesting take on the meaning of the word "perfect":

> *Perfectionism is one of the scariest words I know. It is a marked characteristic of contemporary American culture, a serious psychological affliction that makes people too timid to take necessary risks and causes them to suffer when, although they've done the best they can, their efforts fall short of some imaginary, and usually unattainable standard .... The word that has been translated as "perfect" does not mean to set forth an impossible goal.... It is taken from a Latin word meaning complete, entire, full-grown. To "be perfect," in the sense that Jesus means it, is to make room for growth, for the changes that bring us to maturity, to ripeness.... Perfection, in a Christian sense, means becoming mature to give ourselves to others.* [4]

Another place in the New Testament where the maturity theme

comes to the surface is in Matthew 18:3 – a passage often overlooked or misconstrued. When extracted as a fragment, the verse reads, "Truly I tell you, unless you change and become like children, you will never enter the kingdom of heaven." At first glance, such an admonition seems to contradict the entire premise of these pages. But if Matthew 18:3 is read in relation to the verses that proceed and follow it, it has a meaning almost opposite from when it's read in isolation. This text, *in context,* tells the story of the disciples asking Jesus, "Who is the greatest in the kingdom of heaven?" Jesus calls to a child whom he puts in their midst, and then urges the disciples to "become like children." And then, in the following verse, he explains precisely what he means: "Whoever becomes humble like this child is the greatest in the kingdom of heaven." [5]

Humility is clearly the point of the teaching – not aspiring to a second childhood. Instead of recommending the helplessness and dependency of life's early years, Jesus calls his followers to be adults without arrogance or guile. There is all the difference in the world between *childishness* and *childlikeness.* The invitation is not to mawkish, clinging childishness, but to the childlike humility which comes so naturally to children – a humility that is trusting, receptive, and filled with a sense of wonder. To be in Christ is to be a grown woman, a grown man, taking responsibility for one's self, and exemplifying a humility of vulnerable openness to every person, a willingness to receive people as they are, and a sense of wonderment and awe toward the world around us and the mystery that we call life. It is in this since that Jesus calls us to a maturity that is childlike. [6]

A similar maturity-with-humility theme appears in the writings of the Apostle Paul. In the familiar 13th Chapter of First Corinthians, he discusses the importance of the maturation process and leaving behind certain childish traits. He writes, "When I was a child, I spoke like a child, I thought like a child, I reasoned like a child; when I became an adult, I put an end to childish ways." (13:11) Even though Paul goes on to characterize his maturity as seeing "in a mirror, dimly," his seeing is as an adult and not as a child. He looks forward to a time when "I will know fully, even as I have been fully known." (13:12) This anticipation of the future is not for the sake of reclaiming childish characteristics, but for the sake of one day claiming the full promise of adulthood in Jesus Christ.

Another reference to the subject of maturity – or its absence – is in The Letter to the Hebrews. In the fifth Chapter, the author of the letter chides Jewish Christians for being immature in their failure to understand how Jesus fulfills the role of "priest" (after the order of Melchizedek.) *The J. B. Phillips* translation puts it most vividly:

> *There is a great deal that we should like to say about this high priesthood, but it is not easy to explain it to you since you seem to be slow to grasp spiritual truth. At a time when you should be teaching others, you need teachers yourselves to repeat to you the ABC of God's revelation to men. You have become people who need a milk diet and cannot face solid food! For anyone who continues to live on "milk" – he simply has not grown up. (5:11-13)*

Or, as the Eugene H. Peterson translation of *The Message* has the opening verse in Chapter 6:

> *So come on, let's leave the preschool finger-painting exercises on Christ and get on with the grand work of art. Grow up in Christ.*

These texts remain applicable today to Christians who haven't gone beyond their ABCs or "finger-painting" when it comes to thinking about their relationship to God. Such immaturity isn't due to an inability to grasp more challenging concepts of God; it is due to a preference for a "milk diet" instead of "solid food." After all, there is something childishly appealing about "God the Provider" who furnishes whatever we need, "God the Protector" who hovers over us and intervenes in times of danger, and "God the Problem Solver" who guides and directs us in times of indecision. Ironically, people who hold such views often have college educations and function quite successfully in a world of satellites, computers, spreadsheets and a great array of other sophisticated technologies and systems. But when it comes to thinking about God, the intellectual expectation they choose for themselves is at a kindergarten level.

It isn't that the Gospel is itself, a conundrum of mental complexity. Rather, the conundrum, the complexity, is in us. We wrap ourselves in so many layers of rationalization and denial about the existential threats to our existence – such threats as guilt, death, loss of meaning – it never occurs to us to allow the Christian faith to address these threats and the primal questions they evoke. A religion of warm feelings and easy answers is much preferred. So the child in us, described by Freud as, "destined to remain a child forever," continues clinging to a "cosmic parent" in a scary world.

Notes and References

1. Part I, "Our Oriental Heritage," Simon and Schuster, New York, 1954, p. 63

2. New York, Nashville, Abingdon Press, Vol II, p. 433

3. For further discussion on Christian and Hebrew references to God as "Father," see Amy-Jill Levine, *The Misunderstood Jew*, HarperCollins, 2007, p. 41-45

4. Kathleen Norris, *Amazing Grace*, (New York: Riverhead Books, 1998), p. 55

5. Although this verse is not found in the other gospels, and probably did not originate with Jesus, a number of scholars agree that it likely represents his ideas. It is especially consistent with Jesus' reversal of a child's traditional status in ancient societies as a silent non-participant, along with other instances of his sympathy for outcasts and other marginal people. With this text, and other gospel quotations, I am relying on conclusions arrived at by the scholars in the Jesus Seminar. Their consensus about this text can be found in *The Five Gospels*, Harper Collins Paperback, 1997, p. 89

6. Although the distinction between being *childish* versus being *childlike* is not an explicit distinction in this text, not even a literal reading of the full account would suggest that Jesus is here recommending Christians should be helpless and dependent. Furthermore, the distinction is consistent with the spirit of Jesus advocacy in a number of other instances where he is clearly on the side of healing, wholeness, and what I am calling "coming-of-age."

Chapter II: When Christians Come of Age

Carrying the "Father" Metaphor to Its Logical Conclusion

To what extent then is Freud's analysis of religion still relevant? To what extent are Christians in the United States inclined to think of God primarily as a celestial power watching over them and even intervening on their behalf in times of crises? What is meant when we say, "The Lord will provide," or "God will take care of you," or "We are under a Divine Providence"? Each of these expressions once served as a profound assurance of God's faithfulness toward us – "come what may" – as in the Apostle Paul's affirmation of "nothing in all creation can separate us from the love of God," or in Job's cry, "Though he slay me, I will trust him." The question today is whether such expressions have been reduced to a simplistic *quid pro quo* where having faith in God automatically assures exemption from undesirable and threatening circumstances? If so, such bargaining turns faith into nothing more than an instrumental strategy for achieving practical advantages.

Supernatural Theism

At the national level, when we say or sing, "God Bless America," do we anticipate God literally favoring America as a land of special destiny and privilege – very much as elders bestow favors on their children? How much of our dependency on God is motivated by a hope that in one way or another, God will ease the harsh realities of living in a world of risk and danger? Could it be that our "relationship with God" is nothing more than a projection of the relationship we once enjoyed with earthly parents – authority figures who rescued us when we were in peril, and offered guidance when we needed counsel?

It is my experience that an exceedingly large number of persons attending churches fit Freud's description of "religious people." They believe that God relates to them in an intimately personal way, and that the exigencies of life will somehow be mitigated because of this relationship. Even for those who blanch at the idea of the United States as God's "favorite nation," God is still a personal presence in their lives who, in times of trial and tribulation, will, if not directly intervene, at least impart to them an extra measure of strength and guidance. Such persons mirror what has become the "theologically correct" concept of God in America today, a concept described by New Testament scholar Marcus J. Borg as "Supernatural theism" – the notion of God as a supernatural personal being separate from the world, who is also accessible to persons who meet certain doctrinal requirements and follow certain rituals. [1]

This supernatural theism dominates the large majority of faith communities throughout America. Almost all conservative and evangelical congregations, as well as most mainline Protestant and Roman Catholic churches, reinforce the idea that God is a cosmic problem-solver who comes to the aid of persons who "believe and pray." Such assurances are quite typically the content of countless sermons, hymns and prayers offered on Sunday mornings, and it would be nearly impossible for most congregations to worship any other way.

The God Who "Guides" Us

God is not only seen as favorably changing the course of certain events for religious people, it is believed that "He" even participates in the decision-making process – especially when it comes to making difficult decisions. "Turning to God" is one of the code expressions for persons attempting to solve dilemmas by "seeking the will of God," "being led by the Spirit," and "allowing God to guide and show the way." Just as adolescents are spared the full rigors of adulthood by following the advice and counsel of parents, so too, many Christians seek to avoid the full rigors of maturity and self-reliance by casting God in the role of super parent. Rather than making hard, responsible decisions on their own, facing up to the consequences of those decisions, and trusting that God means for life to come to adults precisely on these terms, they turn religion into a cosmic escape-hatch and regression.

Such decision-making also enjoys the advantage of being quite a power-trip. Directions from a "higher authority" take considerable precedence over mere mortal processes for making up one's mind. In the game of "Spiritual One-up-man-ship," there is no higher trump card than "divine guidance." This, of course, ignores the barbarous consequences such "guidance" has often produced in the past and present. Augusto Pinochet, the Chilean general-turned-dictator who oversaw the torture of some 28,000 and "disappearance" of 3,200 perceived adversaries, told a magazine interviewer, "I get my strength from God." [2] The man who said he would rather see a whole army coming toward him with drawn swords than do battle with one Christian convinced he is about to do the will of God, was a man who knew something about the history of Crusades and other instances of carnage motivated by allegedly religious impulses.

As sociologist Mark Juergensmeyer points out in his book, *Terror in the Mind of God*, "Conflict derived from religious certitude exacerbates the tendency to divide people into friends or enemies, good and evil, us and them. It ratchets up divisions to a cosmic level. What makes religious violence particularly savage and relentless is that it puts worldly conflicts in a larger than life context of cosmic war. Thus, massacres flourish by claiming to be symbolic, absolute and unrestrained by historic circumstances." [3]

I return to the subject of the Iraq war in this chapter not only because it is surely one of the most prominent events of recent decades, but also because President George W. Bush's decision to invade Iraq may well be one of the most flagrant examples of "divinely inspired" horror in America's history. While there is no way of knowing with certainty, the extent to which President Bush presumed to have providential support for his foreign policy, his unmitigated confidence throughout the Iraq campaign leads one to wonder if such absolutism wasn't the result of something more than just following his own best human judgment. (4) At the National Cathedral a few days after 9–11, he claimed a mandate for a fateful agenda: "We are here in the middle hour of our grief. But our responsibility to history is already clear: to answer these attacks and rid the world of evil." The congregation then stood and sang "The Battle Hymn of the Republic." Journalist Bob Woodward wrote that the president "was casting his mission and that of the country in the grand vision of God's master plan." (5) Bush later was reported as saying that God had told him to invade Afghanistan, and then Iraq, and that he had obeyed. (6) This report is consistent with his response nine months after the Iraq incursion when he told an interviewer that he did not turn to his father for strength. "There is," he said, "a higher father that I appeal to." (7)

What a horrendous irony if the instigator of this war – which many now agree was unnecessary and ill conceived – presumes to justify his obstinacy by alleging it was sanctioned on religious grounds. Such a version of the Christian faith can only be described as childishly naive and dangerously simplistic.

I am not suggesting that the Christian faith is silent as a resource for meeting life's uncertainties and problems, nor am I proposing that it is void of values which can assist us in making difficult decisions. Several of the later chapters in this book are about how the Gospel addresses the existential threats to our existence, how conscientious decisions can reflect a Christian morality and ethics, and how prayer can play a role in the lives of persons of faith. What I am suggesting, however, within the family metaphor, is an alternative to casting religious people as quasi-children who project a sentimental father-image to protect and guide them.

Coming-of-Age

Perhaps it never occurred to Freud that religious persons could be mature, self-reliant adults, while also acknowledging God as the ultimate source of their maturity and self-reliance. Within the family metaphor, such persons would be perceived as *grown-up* daughters and sons of a God for whom, humankind, come-of-age, would be as much a goal as it is for earthly parents. In fact, one can't help but wonder how we ever conceived that a "love divine, all loves excelling" would want anything less for creation than the realization of its full potential?

To be sure, there is a stage in child development where parents have a major obligation to provide for needs and the protection of offspring. But being fed, clothed, housed and kept from harm is not the ultimate rationale for human existence. We look with a degree of sadness on the arrested development of children who are physically or emotionally unable to achieve full adulthood. Surely God no more desires the arrested development of human beings than we do of our own sons and daughters.

There is also a stage in maturation called "adolescence" where teenagers try on a variety of personas and experiment with different ways of thinking and being in the world. During this period, the primary role of parents is to offer counsel and advice, attempting to keep sons and daughters from making errors that can be catastrophic, while gently guiding them toward promising life choices. But this is a temporary role. There comes a time when knowledgeable parents no longer intrude with "words of wisdom," allowing offspring to set their own course and begin shaping their own destiny. That time is called "adulthood."

There is something tragically stunted in relationships where parents, long after children are grown, still dominate sons and daughters. Control, manipulation, and holding on through various forms of "emotional blackmail" – these are not the gifts of love; they are the symptoms of a life turned in upon its self. Parents are satisfying their own needs when they make adult offspring helpless and dependent on them. Surely, this is not the need of God, whose *agape* love is unconditional, spendthrift, and poured out without any strings attached. What higher destiny for creation could this love seek than the maturity of responsible, value-driven human beings who not only accept themselves as loved by God, but accept the worth of all persons as beneficiaries of that same love?

There is nothing inevitable about maturity leading to indifference toward one's origin. Creator and creature, like parents and grown children, can continue to be enriched by one another's love, but with a love no longer characterized by dominance and intervention.

A Personal Illustration

My wife and I are the parents of two sons. While they were growing up, we so valued and marveled at each stage of their development that we sometimes spoke wistfully of wishing we could "freeze" them before they reached another stage. This was, of course, hyperbole, and we soon discovered that we were enjoying their most recent spurt of growth as much or more than those that went before.

Today, they are mature men with their own families, and we find ourselves the beneficiaries of adult relationships that provide, in one sense, an even greater satisfaction than we enjoyed while they were growing up. At this stage, we have the privilege of seeing them actualize their manhood and live out, on their own terms and in their own ways, the values that, hopefully, we had some part along the way in shaping.

This does not mean, however, that we and our sons are now indifferent toward each other. Rather, they are still very much a part of us, as we are still very much a part of them. And while our love for them is no less in their maturity than when they were children, we no longer intercede for them or offer our opinions as substitutes for theirs. Our reward is in seeing each son discover his own potential, choose his own vocation, create his own family and friendships, and actualize all the aspects of a uniquely personal life-journey.

If God's love is at all analogous to the experience of a parent's love, then we have downsized love in both instances if it is nothing more than rescue and control. As long as a child's potential is to become a self-reliant person with a passion for justice and the "common good," then surely love – human and divine – includes "giving up childish ways." It must have never occurred to Freud that the *sine qua non* of true religion is not "comparable to a childhood neurosis," but to a religion of maturity, characterized by personal responsibility and social conscience.

Exploring such maturity is the primary focus of the remaining chapters, but I must warn the reader that these chapters will seem credible only in the context of a faith come-of-age, a "Christianity for adults only." This perspective will no longer speak of a direct, intimate, one-on-one relationship with a personal deity (Supernatural theism); instead it will indicate a God disguised in the oblique dynamic of *human relationships*, a dynamic Christians find acted out in the life of Jesus and described in the following two chapters referring to works by Dietrich Bonhoeffer.

Notes and References
1. *The God We Never Knew*, Harper, San Francisco, 1997, p. 17

2. "Chile's Gen. Pinochet, the Strongman Who Tore Apart His Country," Pamela Constable, The Washington Post, 12-12-06, Style, p. 1 & 7

3. *Terror in the Mind of God: The Global Rise of Religious Violence*, University of California Press, 2000, p. 146, 153, 154, 217

4. The certitude of cosmic support was clearly implied in the Bible verses the Pentagon selected for the covers of confidential reports at the start of the Iraq war. Those verses included quotes about putting on "the full armor of God" and seeking divine help, according to GQ magazine. The magazine's Web site features images of covers of the "Worldwide Intelligence Update" from 2003. One report, with a photo of a tank, quotes Ephesians 6:13, which begins, "Therefore put on the full armor of God." Another, with a photo of now-deceased Iraqi president Saddam Hussein, quotes 1 Peter 2:15: "It is God's will that by doing good you should silence the ignorant talk of foolish men." GQ writer, Robert Draper, said

the cover sheet was created by Major General Glen Shaffer, a director of intelligence who reported to both Secretary of Defense Donald Rumsfeld and Joint Chiefs of Staff chair Richard Myers. "When colleagues complained to Shaffer that including a religious message with an intelligence briefing seemed inappropriate, Shaffer politely informed them that the practice would continue, because 'my seniors' – JCS chairman Richard Myers, Rumsfeld, and the commander in chief himself – appreciated the cover pages," Draper wrote.(Christian Century, June 16, 2009, p. 14)

5. *Bush at War*, New York; Simon & Schuster, 2002, p. 67

6. BBC press office. See
http://www.bbc.co.uk/pressoffice/pressreleases/stories/2005/10_october/06/bush.shtml

7. An earlier example of such self deception seems to have occurred in 1999, on the day of Texas' Governor George W. Bush's second inauguration. Richard Land, a longtime leader of the Southern Baptist Convention, sat with the governor on that day, along with several other confidants, and recalls Bush saying, "I believe that God wants me to be president." (The Washington Post Magazine, November 26, 2006, p. 26)

Chapter III: Bonhoeffer on "Religionless Christianity"

Living without God, before God, with God

We turn now to a 20th Century theologian whose theology provides scaffolding for much of this book.

For many Christians the name, Dietrich Bonhoeffer, is synonymous with martyrdom – and rightly so. This remarkable young Lutheran pastor joined the German underground, convinced that it was his duty as a Christian to work for Hitler's defeat. Eventually, he participated in an assassination plot that failed, was arrested and imprisoned, and on April 9, 1945, shortly before Germany's surrender, was executed. He was 39 years old. The account of his life and death is so powerful that, ironically, some of his admirers have allowed it to obscure his extraordinary contribution to Christian thought – especially it's more radical dimensions. That thought, more than any other I am aware of, holds prophetic insights into what it means to live as a mature Christian in a new age.

Some of Bonhoeffer's insights are in the form of hints and clues because much of his work was burned by a Gestapo captain on April 9, 1945, thus leaving only fragmentary and preliminary meditations. But the previous August, in a letter from prison to his dear friend, Eberhard Bethge, he said:

> *I should like to write a book of not more than 100 pages, divided into three chapters:*
>
> *1. A Stocktaking of Christianity.*
>
> *2. The Real Meaning of Christian Faith.*
>
> *3. Conclusions.* [1]

The three chapter titles are then followed by brief, summary paragraphs, constituting little more than an outline of what Bonhoeffer would have written, had he completed the project. While we will never know precisely what he intended, there is enough substantive material in the sketches of these paragraphs to suggest a book proposing a radically new paradigm for Christianity – albeit a paradigm biblically grounded and centered in Christ.

I want to elaborate on the summary paragraphs in each of the three chapters because they approximate so closely the major propositions of this book. At the same time, I am aware of how easy and inappropriate it is to "force" another author's writings to bolster one's own thesis. For this reason I have endeavored to reference much of this chapter with either Bonhoeffer's own words, or with opinions of Bonhoeffer scholars. [2]

"A Stocktaking of Christianity"

Bonhoeffer begins sketching the first chapter of the little book he proposes to write by assuming that his reader is already aware of "The coming of age of mankind." [3] He reminds us that while we can never entirely eliminate "accidents" and "blows of fate," we no longer seek to conquer nature through spiritual means. Our dependency is now on a new environment fashioned by the progress of the western world, and especially its "technical organizations." We have gone from the menace of nature to the menace of technologies, and even though this new environment is our own invention, we have managed to deal with everything except ourselves.

Furthermore, he declares there is now no spiritual force to protect us since "'God' as a working hypothesis, as a stop-gap for our embarrassments, has become superfluous ..." This conclusion reflects some of the content of Bonhoeffer's reading while in prison. During this time, he read Carl-Friedrich von Weizsacker's *On the World-View of Physics* and Zischka's *Science Breaks Monopolies*. These books, along with previous years of conversation with his older brother, Karl-Friedrich, a professor of physical chemistry in Leipzig, led him to declare, "We are to find God in what we know, not in what we don't know..." (4)

Also, while in prison, he read the philosopher Wilhelm Dilthey. Dilthey argued that human beings began thinking autonomously from the time of the Renaissance and the Reformation, using autonomous reason to explain politics, law, natural sciences and other subjects. Bonhoeffer agrees with Dilthey, and this agreement is reflected in one of his prison letters on the same subject:

> *I'll try to define my position from the historical angle. The movement that began about the thirteenth century... towards the autonomy of man (in which I should include the discovery of the laws by which the world lives and deals with itself in science, social and political matters, art, ethics, and religion) has in our time reached an undoubted completion. Man has learnt to deal with himself in all questions of importance without recourse to the "working hypothesis" called "God." In questions of science, art, and ethics this has become an understood thing at which one now hardly dares to tilt. But for the last hundred years or so it has become increasingly true of religious questions; it is becoming evident that everything gets along without "God" – and, in fact, just as well as before. As in the scientific field, so in human affairs generally, "God" is being pushed more and more out of life, losing more and more ground.* (5)

Bonhoeffer considers the "man who has become of age" to be "religionless." By "religionless" he does not necessarily mean without faith. By this time, he had arrived at a negative interpretation of "religion," and used it as a pejorative word in the way understood by Barth when he declared in an essay: "Jesus has nothing to do with religion." (6) According to Ralph K. Wustenberg, Bonhoeffer started with a positive view of "religion," due to the influence of liberal theology; and under Karl Barth, moved to a critical interpretation. But by the time he was imprisoned, he assumed that "religion" was finished, and he became an advocate for what he called "religionless Christianity." (7)

Bonhoeffer now saw the Church as an anachronism and its piet-
ism "as a last effort to maintain evangelical Christianity as a religion." He
believed Lutheran orthodoxy had become an "attempt to rescue the
Church as an institution for salvation," and that even the Confessing
Church was more characterized by standing up for the Church's "cause"
than by its personal faith in Christ. He was particularly disappointed by
the Confessing Church's failure to risk itself as an advocate for the Jews.
Sociologically, he saw the institutional church as almost exclusively iden-
tified with the upper and middle classes, always on the defensive, and
never taking chances. It had little or no effect on the great majority of
people and public morality.

Since the church is crumbling under the weight of its own desperate attempts at self-survival, Bonhoeffer recommends that Christians, at
the moment, can only keep the secret disciplines of prayer and righteous
action, and wait for a new day – which may even include, a new, "non-
religious" language. Furthermore, behind his analysis of a "world come-
of-age" is the premise that it is God who has created us to live without
the "God hypothesis," and that the silence evoked by such a void – is of
God.

"The Real Meaning of Christian Faith"

The outline for the second chapter builds on the idea that not even
"the secular" can escape from God, and that we experience authentic
transcendence when we exist for others – thereby participating in the being of Jesus. In a July 21, 1944 letter, Bonhoeffer wrote:

> *I am still discovering right up to this moment, that it is only by living*
> *completely in this world that one learns to have faith. One must com-*
> *pletely abandon any attempt to make something of oneself, whether it be*
> *a saint, or a converted sinner, or a churchman (a so-called priestly type!),*
> *a righteous man or an unrighteous one, a sick man or a healthy one. By*
> *this-worldliness I mean living unreservedly in life's duties, problems,*
> *successes and failure, experiences and perplexities. In so doing we throw*

ourselves completely into the arms of God, taking seriously, not our own suffferings, but those of God in the world - watching with Christ in Gethsemane. That is how one becomes a man and a Christian. [8]

Jesus is seen, not as *a* man, but as *the* man whose significance is defined by his "being there for others." Faith is knowing that our relationship to God "...is not a 'religious' relationship to the highest, most powerful, and best Being imaginable..." but rather a relation to "...a new life in 'existence for others,' through participation in the being of Jesus." The transcendent is never distant or unattainable; it is with "the neighbour who is within reach in any given situation." God in human form is not some metaphysical alchemy of divinity mixed with humanity, but rather God the Crucified, "the man for others," who experiences the transcendent through relationships with other human beings. [9]

In other writings, Bonhoeffer discusses Christ's divinity as being hidden. He insists that there is no work of Christ that is unequivocal; it all remains open to ambiguous interpretations. Jesus can be seen as hero, or as a brave man, or as a miracle worker in a land of miracle workers and healers. "There is no point in the life of Jesus, to which one could point and say clearly, 'Jesus here was indubitably the Son of God,' ... No, he did his work in the incognito of history, in the flesh." [10]

Even the resurrection is not a penetration of the incognito. Even the resurrection is ambiguous. It is only believed in where the stumbling block of Jesus has not been removed. Only the disciples who followed Jesus saw the resurrection. Only blind faith sees here. [11]

So, for Bonhoeffer, faith is participation in a new life centering in "existence for others," and thereby, a participation in the incarnation, cross and resurrection of Jesus.

This second chapter contains only the briefest reference to Bonhoeffer's intention to write about how his Christology is the basis for interpreting other biblical concepts (Creation, fall, atonement, repentance, faith, the new life, and the last things.) He also plans a section on "cultus" and "religion." But the final section in this chapter deals with, "What do we really believe?"

He laments that "belief" is too often a *content* question, as in "Must I believe in the Apostles Creed?" Lutherans, the Reformed Churches, Roman Catholics, and the Confessing Church itself – all seem preoccupied with doctrines, creeds, and other *content* considerations. For this man, who in his own death acted out what it means to have faith, the authentic and inescapable question of human existence is not grounded in what *content* one ascribes to, but in the *existential question*: "What do we really believe? I mean, believe in such a way that we stake our lives on it?" He acknowledges that *content* considerations have their place, "... but they do not absolve us from the duty of being honest with ourselves." And then, if the reader wants to know more precisely what he means, he refers us back to the previous part of the chapter which centers on a life transformed by its encounter with *the man* who lived his life and died his death for others.

In other letters and writings, Bonhoeffer elaborates on how a life can be transformed by Christ, yet lived entirely in the secular world. And, in the next chapter, we will consider how the decision-making process is itself a part of that transformation. But it is also important to understand that the transformation, if complete, frees one from any preoccupation with being "religious." He says, "The 'religious act' is always something partial; 'faith' is something whole, involving the whole of one's life. Jesus calls men, not to a new religion, but to life." (12) Liberated from false religious obligations, one may now live a "secular life."

It would be an error to mistake Bonhoeffer's "secular life" for a life of profligacy or ease. The life of which he speaks is determined by a Christological framework. He does not mean "the shallow and banal this-worldliness of the enlightened, the busy, the comfortable, or the lascivious, but a profound this-worldliness characterized by discipline and the constant knowledge of death and resurrection." [13] It is a life of paradox, of waiting for God on the one hand, while praying and actively doing good on the other hand. Under these circumstances, according to Lutheran scholar, Frits de Lange:

> *...there is only one way left to be religious; it is in recognizing that one can be no longer religious in the traditional sense of that word. According to Bonhoeffer, the only good Christian is a "worldly" Christian who takes without reservation, her or his responsibilities in building up a just and humane society.* [14]

"Conclusions"

The outline for this third and final chapter is about the Church and matters pertaining to its ministry and mission. Toward the end of the chapter, Bonhoeffer declares, "...there are certain things that I am anxious to say simply and clearly ..." [15] One is not likely to find any statement on the church put more "simply" or "clearly" than:

> *The Church is the Church only when it exists for others. To make a start, it should give away all its property to those in need. The clergy must live solely on the free-will offerings of their congregations, or possibly engage in some secular calling. The Church must share in the secular problems of ordinary human life, not dominating, but helping and serving. It must tell men of every calling what it means to live in Christ, to exist for others.* [16]

He then precedes to a critique of the Church that he knows best – the Church of his own Lutheran tradition. And, once again, without mincing words, he warns against "the vices of *hubris*, power-worship, envy, and humbug, as the roots of all evil." [17] He extols virtues of "... moderation, purity, loyalty, constancy, patience, discipline, humility, contentment, and modesty," [18] and the reader can't help but lament the lost opportunity to ponder Bonhoeffer's elaboration on these words, had he lived long enough to write about them.

The outline points to the significance of a human example, which has its origin in the humanity of Jesus, and is emphasized in Paul's teaching. The proclamation of the Christian faith has never been located in generalities, but always in the particular and the specific; "....it is not abstract argument, but example, that gives its word emphasis and power." [19] Bonhoeffer regrets a loss in the church's emphasis on "example," and expresses the hope of later taking up this subject and its place in the New Testament. He also looks forward to writing on the question of revising the creeds (especially the Apostles' Creed) and Christian apologetics, as well as reforming the training of clergy and the pattern of clerical life. [20]

Having called for Christians to live a secrete discipline of praying and doing good, while waiting in silence for God's Word, one might easily conclude that Bonhoeffer expects the institutional church to all but disappear. However, if that were the case, there would be no need for him to write this final chapter. He is clearly interested in reforming the institution, reclaiming its servant role, recovering the importance of example, revising creeds and apologetics, and renewing the life of the clergy. Bonhoeffer's church, whether gathering in homes, store fronts, offices, or other "secular" places, would still occupy real space and be composed of a body of people.

Even though the outline for this third chapter ends with only the briefest reference to the importance of the church's physical presence in the world, Bonhoeffer did elaborate in other writings on various dimensions of its institutional nature. As to occupying space he wrote:

> ...the Incarnation does involve a claim to a space of its own on earth. Anything which claims space is visible. Hence the Body of Christ can only be a visible Body, or else it is not a Body at all. [21]

He further contends:

> A truth, a doctrine, or a religion needs no space for themselves. They are disembodied entities. But the incarnate Son of God needs not only ears

and hearts, but living men who will follow him. That is why he called his disciples into a literal, bodily following, and thus made his fellowship with them a visible reality. (22)

For Bonhoeffer, the Church is the visible body of the exalted Lord where the Word of God is spoken through the human word. This Word, spoken by the Apostles, exists of its own accord, and all the preacher has to do is to assist its delivery, and put no obstacle in its path. It cannot exist without the humanity it has assumed, for it is the "Word made flesh" – proclaiming what it means to be human in the fullest and deepest sense. (23)

The task of preaching, (what Luther called "the little sacrament"), is not the only means whereby the Church takes visible form. In the sacraments of Baptism and the Eucharist, we receive the Body of Christ. Baptism makes us members of the Body, and the Lord's Supper confers bodily fellowship with Christ and with each other. The spoken Word is for the world, believers and unbelievers, while the two sacraments belong exclusively to the church since, through them, we symbolically identify ourselves with "the man for others." (24)

In other writings, Bonhoeffer made clear his sensitivity to the fragility of Christian community, and how readily human beings predicate the church on something other than the grace of God. With great sociological and psychological insight, he warned that a community is not an ideal, not a longed-for psychic reality to work toward and obtain. As with a marriage, so with a congregation; forgiveness is the linchpin of all community.

I want to quote at some length from his *Life Together* because, for 46 years of serving congregations, I found this passage profoundly relevant in times of great harmony and in times of crisis. At least once a year, from the pulpit of each of the churches I served, I made it a point to remind the congregation of the one essential insight upon which Christian fellowship depends. I read these words aloud:

Innumerable times a whole Christian community has broken down because it had sprung from a wish dream. The serious Christian, set down for the first time in a Christian community, is likely to bring with him a very definite idea of what Christian life together should be and to try to realize it. But God's grace speedily shatters such dreams. Just a surely as God desires to lead us to a knowledge of genuine Christian fellowship, so surely must we be overwhelmed by a great disillusionment with others, with Christians in general, and, if we are fortunate, with ourselves.

By sheer grace, God will not permit us to live even for a brief period in a dream world. He does not abandon us to those rapturous experiences and lofty moods that come over us a like a dream. God is not a God of the emotions but the God of truth. Only that fellowship which faces such disillusionment, with all its unhappy and ugly aspects, begins to be what it should be in God's sight, begins to grasp in faith the promise that is given to it... He who loves his dream of a community more than the Christian community itself becomes a destroyer of the latter, even though his personal intentions may be ever so honest and earnest and sacrificial.

Thus the very hour of disillusionment with my brother becomes incomparably salutary, because it so thoroughly teaches me that neither of us can ever live by our own words and deeds, but only by the one Word and Deed which really binds us together - the forgiveness of sins in Jesus Christ. When the morning mists of dreams vanish, then dawns the bright day of Christian fellowship. (25)

Bonhoeffer concludes the outline for a little book he will never live to write with, "I hope it may be of some help for the Church's future." Believing that we are already living in a world "come-of-age," "without God, before God, with God," he stubbornly insists on the imperative of the physical presence of the church, the body of Christ, as a sign that even the absence of God is a God-shaped absence. (26) The community that bears this witness depends utterly on forgiveness – individuals forgiving as they have been forgiven.

Notes and References

1. Dietrich Bonhoeffer, *Letters and Papers from Prison*, Revised Edition, Edited by Eberhard Bethge, The Macmillan Company, New York, p. 200 - 201

2. I am particularly indebted to the scholars writing in *Bonhoeffer for a New Day*, Edited by John W. De Gruchy. This book is a compilation of papers presented at the Seventh International Bonhoeffer Congress held in Cape Town in 1996.

3. Like other theologians of his day, Bonhoeffer used the words "man" and "mankind" as generic references – not intended to be gender specific. Had he lived to see the movement toward inclusive language, I am confident he would have been in its vanguard.

4. Op. Cit., p. 164

5. Ibid., p. 167-168

6. Karl Barth, "Das Wort Gottes und die Theologie," Munich 1924, p. 94

7. *Bonhoeffer for a New Day*, Ralph K. Wustenberg, "Bonhoeffer's Tegel Theology", Op. Cit., p. 59

8. Ibid., p. 193

9. Ibid., p. 202

10. Dietrich Bonhoeffer, *Christ the Center*, Harper and Row, New York, 1960, p.39

11. Ibid., p. 116

12. *Letters and Papers from Prison*, Op. Cit., p. 191

13. Ibid., p. 193

14. Frits de Lange, "The Churches' Embarrassment in Speaking about

God," *Bonhoeffer for a New Day*, Op. Cit., p. 111

15. *Letters and Papers from Prison*, Op. Cit., p. 204

16. Ibid., p. 203-204

17. Ibid., p. 204

18. Ibid., p. 204

19. Ibid., p.204

20. Ibid., p. 204

21. *The Cost of Discipleship*, The Macmillan Company, New York, 1949, p. 223

22. Ibid., p. 223

23. Ibid., p. 225

24. Ibid., p. 225-226

25. *Life Together*, Harper & Brothers, New York, 1954, p. 26 - 29

26. This view has much in common with *via negativa* theology which assumes that God can only be described in terms of what God is not. However, for Bonhoeffer, the hidden God is found in "the man for others" who both reveals and conceals the divine reality.

Chapter IV: Bonhoeffer's Ethics

Making Ethical Decisions without "Divine Guidance"

To propose that God calls Christians to live in the world come-of-age without supernatural interventions or divinely-inspired directions, immediately provokes questions as to how we go about solving ethical dilemmas. Stripped of all absolutes and the assurances which accompany them, how do mature women and men of faith engage the decision-making process with the intention of doing the will of God? In fact, what is the "will of God" in such a world, and how should we proceed in matters of ethical concern?

As in the previous chapter, I want to draw on a number of insights from Dietrich Bonhoeffer. However, in this instance, my source is a compilation of writings, some preliminary and some complete, which he succeeded in hiding in a garden before he was arrested and imprisoned. They were written between 1940 and 1943, and while Bonhoeffer considered a number of possible titles for this work, his sub-title was: "A Tentative Christian Ethic." [1] Here again, his dear friend, Eberhard Bethge, edited the compilation, and it was published under the title, *Ethics*. [1] We will not attempt to cover all the subjects discussed in the work, but will focus primarily on the dynamics of the decision-making process for ethical dilemmas.

Where to Begin?

Bonhoeffer proposes that most of us approach an ethical problem with the hope of *being good* and *doing good.* However, in both instances, the attempt is to satisfy something from within ourselves: the hope of *being good* and *doing good.* Invariably, the premise of our ethical concerns rests on a preoccupation with our selves and with the world.

Allow me to offer several examples from my own experience to illustrate what he means. The dilemma of how much of one's disposable income to allocate to the church and/or charitable causes is a dilemma for my wife and me, as it is for most Christians. We are inclined to approach the issue out of the hope of being good by excelling in generosity and doing good through making wise and prudent contributions. But when it comes to generosity, how much is enough? Granted we have the biblical standard of the tithe, but is that ten percent of one's gross or net income? Before taxes or after? What portion do we give to the church and what portion to charities? What are the criteria?

Similarly with doing good and making the world better than we found it. Most church budgets support benevolent and charitable services, and a portion of what we pay in income tax finds its way to certain social and welfare projects. We receive, on a weekly average, at least three appeals from what appear to be worthy charities and eleemosynary institutions. How do we leverage and maximize our giving to its fullest potential, determining which of many options will be the greatest benefit to humankind?

Our experience is that such questions never get answered completely. We are left invariably with a feeling of slight uncertainty, the vague unease that whatever we decide will not quite fulfill our hope of being as good as we would like to be, or of doing all the good that we would like to do.

A similar dilemma confronts us when we consider the allocation of time. How can we be good and do good in filling obligations to family, work, church, politics and various volunteer organizations, as well as obligations to ourselves as individuals? Who of us ever feels that we have devoted sufficient time to all the worthy responsibilities and duties that impinge upon our lives? We simply do the best we can, and when it comes to justifying the priorities we have chosen, there are several explanations we are inclined to offer.

Bonhoeffer deals with the appeal to *motives* as one of the ways we exonerate ourselves in the decision-making process. Often we are inclined to say, "My intentions were good," or, "I was sincerely trying to help," or, "I followed my heart." But on what basis do we conclude that *motive* is the ultimate ethical justification? He argues, "... a 'good' motive may spring from a very dark background of human consciousness and un-consciousness..." and "...a 'good' attitude may be the source of the worst of actions." [2] Many of our motives come from deeply buried experiences in a past we have long forgotten or repressed; they have their origins in complexities we will never understand. My parents loved me with a love infused with the very best of intentions, but for all their efforts, they still left some scars on my psyche. And I, like my parents, have loved my sons with a love that, in spite of itself, passed some of those same scars on to them, along with some new scars as well. And my sons have done the same with their own children. Who of us has not acted out of the sincerest of *motives*, only to discover that the results were not always what we intended?

Similarly with *conscience* - like *motive*, it is derived from a depth which lies beyond both will and reason. It exists for the sake of preserving the unity of the self, and our natural human inclination is to locate the unity of the self in being right. This means that we come to each ethical decision with the assumption that we have knowledge of good and evil, right and wrong, and that we can maintain the unity of the self by deciding and acting accordingly. Thus we are involved in "highly-principled" actions as a result of "following our *conscience*," and thereby we satisfy the ego's need for self-justification. But since the *conscience* reflects the mores, laws and traditions that have, from early on, shaped and molded us, we end up finding the unity of the self in culturally determined rules and regulations which, themselves, evolve and change from within a culture, as well as differing between cultures.

Bonhoeffer also discusses the appeal to *consequences* as a rationale for decision-making -- the exoneration of one's choices on the basis of outcomes and results. But when we try to trace outcomes and results, he argues, they "... finally disappear from view in the mists of the future." [3] How often an action appears to have a favorable result one day, only to take on the characteristics of a mistake the next day! And what appears as a mistake on that day, yields positive benefits we could not foresee until a month later. And what appears to be working out a month later, can, in the long run, cause others' unintended pain and anguish. And after that …? *Consequences* are ephemeral vagabonds that keep moving on *ad infinitum*. How far do you get to follow them to determine you made the "right decision?" It's like following the proverbial elephant to its grave-yard. You can't get there from here.

For Bonhoeffer, it isn't that *motive, conscience* and *consequences* aren't important, but they are secondary. The ultimate criterion for judging what constitutes Christian decision-making lies elsewhere.

How to Decide

> *Whoever wishes to take up the problem of a Christian ethic must be confronted at once with a demand which is quite without parallel. He must from the outset discard as irrelevant the two questions which alone impel him to concern himself with the problem of ethics, 'How can I be good?' and 'How can I do good?', and instead of these he must ask the utterly and totally different question 'What is the will of God?'* [4]

So, what does it mean to ask "What is the will of God" in a world come- of-age where the God hypothesis is irrelevant? How do we look for "the will of God" in a place where even God is absent?

As discussed in the previous chapter, Bonhoeffer finds God revealed in *the* human being, Jesus Christ. Jesus is the example of what it means to be human in the most authentic sense, which is to say, in him, we see what it means to do "the will of God." And what we see in Jesus, on the one hand, is a man who makes decisions with a profound sense of *obligation* to his own Jewish tradition: The Talmud, The Decalogue, and the prophets. "Do not think that I have come to abolish the law or the prophets; I have come not to abolish but to fulfill." (5) So he is not an anarchist or a law unto himself. Commandments and ethical precedents matter.

On the other hand, and at the same time, Jesus lives with a profound sense of his *freedom*. On occasions, out of that freedom, he goes against the law, and encourages his disciples to do the same. Nothing absolutely compels or coerces him to choose to act a certain way. He is not a slave, not a puppet, there are no strings attached to him, manipulated by a cosmic puppeteer. Not even his crucifixion is scripted or foreordained. No one takes his life from him; he lays it down of his own accord. The only boundaries that he experiences as limitations are the same finite boundaries that limit every human being.

Jesus' choice to obey or disobey a law is predicated on taking that law into himself, rigorously weighing its implications, measuring its claims against other claims, and considering it out of what Bonhoeffer calls Jesus' "own most personal knowledge." The phrase, "own most personal knowledge," does not refer to secret insights or mystical answers unavailable to other mortals. Rather, it is Bonhoeffer's way of referring to the inevitable tension which exists between *freedom* and *obligation*, a tension which can be found in every person who weighs seriously moral and ethical dilemmas. It is in such a tension – and only such a tension – that there is forged what Bonhoeffer calls "responsible decisions." (6)

This process of decision-making is accessible to every Christian. For us, Jesus is the Christ, not because he is unlike us, but because, as our "elder brother," he shows the way and demonstrates what it means to make responsible decisions in the context of being fully mature. No one put it better than Joseph Wesley Mathews when he said of Jesus:

> *I mean he lived his life, and experienced death even as anyone else, save he seemed to <u>really</u> live his. However one chooses to account for it – special mutations of genes, unusual neurotic tendencies, peculiar*

environmental influences, unique occurrences of lucidity – is all quite
beside my concern at the moment. Here was one who apparently not on-
ly lived, but <u>lived</u> his living. (7)

This is another way of saying he was "perfectly human," living to
the fullest extent out of his finite capacity to make *responsible* decisions
forged in the crucible of tension between a sense of *freedom* and a sense of
obligation. Or, one could say that such decision-making was Jesus way of
recreating the commandments out of himself.

Bonhoeffer offers the commandment, "You shall not commit adultery," as an illustration:

If I love my wife, if I accept marriage as an institution of God, then there
comes an inner freedom and certainty of life and action in marriage; I no
longer watch with suspicion every step that I take; I no longer call in
question every deed that I perform. The divine prohibition of adultery is
then no longer the centre around which all my thought and action in
marriage revolves. (As though the meaning and purpose of marriage con-
sisted of nothing except the avoidance of adultery!) But it is the honoring
and the free acceptance of marriage, the leaving behind of the prohibition
of adultery, which is now the pre condition for the fulfillment of the di-
vine commission of marriage. The divine commandment has here become
the permission to live in marriage in freedom and certainty. (8)

To be faithful in a marriage only because there is a commandment
against adultery is blind compliance. And, to be unfaithful in a marriage
simply because one has the freedom to keep or break the marriage vow is
to dishonor both the vow and the person to whom it is made. Authentic
faithfulness in marriage is found in freely choosing faithfulness with open
eyes and a joyous heart. While honoring the institution and the beloved,
it is a way of recreating the commandment out of one's self.

I mentioned earlier Bonhoeffer's well-known expression of living
"without God, before God, with God." I believe that is precisely how Je-

sus lived, and why he is the perfect model of what it means to be an authentic human being. He lived "without God" in the sense that he did not expect God to intervene in his behalf or to make decisions for him. His choices were framed in a psyche of full human consciousness; Jesus was free to choose among multiple alternatives and options. While in every sense a man of his own time and culture, taking seriously his Jewish roots and the political realities of his day, there was no external power arbitrarily controlling him.

But to say that Jesus lived "without God" does not preclude the reality that he also lived "before God." He knew that his autonomy was from the Source of all good gifts, that his freedom was the gracious offering of a Supreme Love, and that he was created in God's image to be creative and generative in his own decision-making. Each of his decisions was offered up to the Mystery which created him to experience his life as a decision-making process. Even in his darkest moments, in his deepest doubts, he never lost the consciousness of anguishing and doubting "before God."

Furthermore, while living "without God" and "before God," Jesus lived "with God." As "the man for others," he was God's presence in the world – caring, healing, loving – the Mystery Incarnate. God came into the world through him. And, while recognizing the presence of God in himself, he recognized that same presence in every other person. He lived as though the "personal" was God's incognito, and that through relationships he touched the eternal in both himself and others. His love, revealing God's love, turned out to be suffering and sacrificial. This was not because "blood sacrifice" was required by some metaphysical judicial power, but because, as every parent and lover knows, the very nature of love is to be suffering and sacrificial. Jesus not only lived "without God" and "before God," he lived "with God" present in himself and others. And thereby became our template for what it means to be faithfully, truly human.

Ethics in a New Key

With Christ as his center, Bonhoeffer set out to write a new ethics for a new time. It was not ethics taken up with concrete problems evoking "ethical solutions." Neither was it a compilation of "ethical principles" to be applied to various issues. Rather, it was ethics basically without content; it focused on the renewal of human relationships in Christ and on the radical demands of love which such relationships require. The secondary influences of *motive, conscience* and *consequences* were surely involved, but the primary aim was to do the will of God as Jesus did, making *responsible* decisions in the polarity between *freedom* and *obligation*. Such decisions are never made "in general" or in the abstract; they are always forged in specific regard to strangers, friends, "enemies," family, church, vocation, nation, and every aspect of existence where choices are required.

Bonhoeffer also knew that some uncertainty was the one, overriding characteristic of such decision-making, and that this uncertainty meant living without assurances that one was being good or doing good in a moralistic, legalistic sense. In the real world, the Christian does not enjoy the luxury of aspiring to be righteous, but only hopes to approximate *responsible* decisions, and to depend ultimately on grace. This means living with anguish, struggle, relativity, compromise and danger. The cost can be high.

Bonhoeffer's own decision to live in a world of ambiguity and uncertainty cost him not only his life; but with some people, his reputation as a Christian pastor. Upon learning of his participation in the plot to assassinate Hitler, many of his friends questioned how he could be so devoted to the principles of non-violence, and yet willfully contribute to a plan for taking another human life? But this is precisely where Bonhoeffer believed a new ethics for a new day would lead: into the very jaws of experiences no longer offering the luxury of clear-cut choices.

Obedience to God means acting without knowledge of the absolute efficacy of one's actions. And, the only way one can possibly live with such nearly unbearable uncertainty is by trusting that whatever else is implied by the symbolic letters, "G-O-D," there is a merciful transcendent love. Trusting this love, alone, is what made it possible for Saint Augustine to cry, "Love God, and do as you please." Or, as Martin Luther urged: "Sin bravely."

Dynamics of a Christian Decision

Since we experience our obligation to God and neighbor through the claims of covenants, laws and commandments, we have to pick and choose, compromise and prioritize. Our problem is not that we don't know what our obligations are; our problem is we have so many.

The dilemma of allocating certain portions of one's disposable income to charities and churches, while providing for one's own insurance, medical care, food, clothing, shelter, etc. is complicated by the fact that these obligations constitute a multiplicity of worthy options. Such options are made all the more worthy by a theological understanding of creation as "very good," which means that caring for our own basic human needs and other necessities can be just as responsible as humanitarian provisions for others. And John Wesley's admonition, "Gain all you can. Save all you can. Give all you can.," still leaves unsolved the specific quandary of how to arrive at allocations in the family budget. As Christians, and especially as affluent Christians, we cannot escape the weight and burden of such heavy financial obligations.

At the same time, to be "truly free," is to weigh these obligations in the knowledge that they are unrelieved by any exception, rationalization or extenuating circumstance. Our obligation to God and neighbor is an absolute imperative that does not release us to pat solutions or self-justifying formulas. The person who is "truly free," is the person who feels the tension between freedom and obligation, and in that tension, makes the most responsible decision he or she can make. This act includes, as well, the offering of that decision to God, accepting the consequences of the decision, and moving on in life to make the next decision and the next.

Included in such decision-making is the knowledge that saying "yes" to one obligation usually means saying "no" to other obligations. Your decision to read this book at this time automatically excludes your reading any other book at this same time. Your decision to be at a particular geographic place precludes the possibility of being at any other geographic place. We live within a finite matrix of time, gravity and spatial limitations that define the scope of all our options.

The tension in ethical decision-making is further characterized by hard-to-face realties. For instance, when I decide to eat, I decide to let another person starve. This may sound melodramatic, but it is literally and irrefutably true. I could, at any time, skip a meal and send its cost to organizations that feed the hungry. Responsible decisions are not exempt from leaving other responsible options unfulfilled. What seems a worthy choice may well preclude other less worthy choices, just as what seems a tragic choice may well appear as only less tragic than other choices. Therefore, Bonhoeffer contends:

> *The action of the responsible man is performed in the obligation which alone gives freedom and which gives entire freedom, the obligation to God and to our neighbor as they confront us in Jesus Christ. At the same time it is performed wholly within the domain of relativity, wholly in the twilight which the historical situation spreads over good and evil; it is performed in the midst of the innumerable perspectives in which every given phenomenon appears. It has not to decide simply between right and wrong and between good and evil, but between right and right and between wrong and wrong.* [9]

An absolute "good" is now no longer understood as one of the options in the dichotomy between "good and evil." To claim that we have ultimate knowledge in this dichotomy is indeed to eat of the fruit which presumes we can "... be like God, knowing good and evil." [10] Only when we surrender this claim can we then reclaim the "good" in its original meaning as derived from the root word, "God." Then, says Bonhoeffer, we can speak of the "guidance of God," not as a cosmic clue to certitude, but as God's own intent for us to live in the tension of making responsible decisions forged in freedom and obligation, and submitted as our relative best effort. In fact, Bonhoeffer even calls such an effort "the deed of God." In doing it, you are doing precisely what God intends. [11]

Who, then, Needs Prayer?

Inevitably, in light of the above understanding, the question is raised, "What is the purpose of prayer? Why pray at all?" To be sure, as long as prayer is envisioned as a means to an end, as a technique for persuading a supernatural power to have a change of mind and do something which that power would not ordinarily do – such prayers will hold little if any meaning for Christians come-of-age. Bonhoeffer, himself a man of prayer, felt that it cheapens and trivializes prayer to appeal to the "god of the gaps."

The theologian I found most helpful in addressing the subject of prayer was Carl Michalson, whose last book was published after his untimely death in a plane crash in 1965. The book was entitled *Worldly Theology*. [12] With such a theology as his premise, this Professor of Systematic Theology at Drew School of Theology preached a number of sermons on the subject of prayer. Following his death, the sermons were collected and published by The Carl Michalson Society at Drew University, Madison, New Jersey.

One of the sermons is entitled, "Can Modern Man Any Longer Pray?" Michalson sees the cry of Jesus from the cross, "My God, why has thou forsaken me?" as:

> ...*the announcement of the new age of maturity that has only begun to catch up with us in the modern world. God who loves us, forsakes us – as the very ground of our responsibility for the world. Then you might ask, how can man any longer pray under these circumstances? So we're re-*

sponsible for the world – why pray? Well, you should know one thing. You would no longer pray in an effort to ask <u>God</u> to do what he has already asked <u>you</u> to do. (13)

He then suggests that a prayer of thanksgiving, rather than focusing on petty comforts and minutiae, or offering flattering utterances of praise to God, would thank God for making each of us responsible for the world and for the obligation that we now have to shape the course of modern history. Or, as Meister Eckhart put it: "If the only prayer you say in your life is thank you, that would suffice." Michalson further suggests that a prayer of confession, rather than admitting to impieties, naughty actions and an unending list of character flaws, would confess "the only sin there is – default in responsibility for God's world." (14)

In another sermon, entitled, "How Working People Can 'Pray Without Ceasing,'" Michalson quotes Gerhard Ebeling in saying that the very meaning of life is "praying without ceasing." By that, he doesn't mean that just any thing we do is automatically religious. But he does mean that:

You don't rob time from life to be holy. Life as it is meant to be lived is itself an act of prayer. How do we understand that? An act of prayer is every act in which we are receiving the world from God as our responsibility. That's not something you do verbally, but rather actively. (15)

In the same sermon, he speaks of intercessory prayer as our way of sighing over the wretchedness we encounter at an individual level, as well as the privation we know exists throughout the world. Yet with these sighs, and with hands outstretched toward situations too heavy for us to cope with, we nevertheless assume the Herculean responsibility of doing all we can to relieve suffering and injustice. The sermon concludes with Michalson's own hope that each of us in Christ will live and pray in such a way that living and praying will "become one – indistinguishably fused." (16)

All of this suggests that prayer is not something we say, but something we become. Nowhere, I believe, is the question, "Why pray?" better answered than in these words by the late Ira G. Zepp, Jr. In the "Introduction" to a collection of his prayers published after he retired as Professor of Religious Studies at McDaniel College (formerly Western Maryland College), Westminster, Maryland, Zepp wrote:

> *...the answer to prayer is not words, but more of God in our life, more of love, more of joy, more of power, more of meaning, a fuller self which more adequately reflects the One in whose image we are made. What better answer could there be to prayer?* [17]

An Example

I once counseled with a couple who had a very dear and loving Down's syndrome child, as well as several other children without special needs. Because the little girl had reached a certain age, the parents had to decide whether to place her in an institution where, during the week, she would live and go to school with other Down's syndrome children, or to bring in a special teacher to provide home-schooling. At stake was not only the welfare of that child, but the effects of either arrangement on their other children. The parents had also to consider their own schedules, transportation arrangements, and the financial resources upon which they could draw in planning for either option.

During my conference with them, they told me of consulting several physicians with expertise in Down syndrome. Those physicians offered different recommendations. They talked with parents of other Down syndrome children who had faced similar dilemmas, only to discover some favored institutional schooling while others preferred a home arrangement. After reading a number of books on the subject, and reflecting on all the information they had gathered, the parents were still undecided.

They came to confer with me, their pastor. After listening to them describe in some detail their search for an appropriate solution, and after asking a few clarifying questions, I empathized with them over the uncertainties that either option seemed to offer. Then, rather than posing as one in possession of some privileged insight, or as one who could lead them in a prayer that would produce an exit strategy out of their dilemma, I decided to share with them Dietrich Bonhoeffer's perspective on what it means to make decisions as mature Christians in the modern world. They listened intently, made thoughtful responses, and appeared to welcome a point of view they had never heard before.

As we concluded the session, it seemed appropriate to ritualize what we had been discussing by placing it in the context of a prayer. We didn't ask God to advise them, or to relieve them as parents from the stress of making a hard decision. Instead, we prayed that, having weighed all their options, they would arrive at the wisest decision they were capable of making. And, after that, as they lived with whatever unknown consequences lay ahead, we prayed that they would surrender their decision to the grace of God, and move on to make future, difficult decisions. We closed with words of gratitude for being created in a world where so much of our destiny is in our hands, and where we can pray as Christians come-of-age.

In a word, we joined Bonhoeffer in his wondrously outrageous claim that through the process of weighing *freedom* and *obligations*, we can make *responsible* decisions that represent "the will of God." And, through such decisions, we even participate in what pastor Bonhoeffer called a "deed of God."

In concluding this chapter, I want to acknowledge that all its illustrations pertain to individual, personal morality and ethics. I have omitted examples of what it would mean to make *responsible* decisions regarding controversial social issues because I believe applying Bonhoeffer's ethics to such issues deserves a chapter of its own. The following pages will allow us to view the subjects of abortion, homosexuality, gun control and war from within the dialectical perspective of Bonhoeffer's *freedom* and *obligation.*

Notes and References

1. Dietrich Bonhoeffer, The Macmillan Company, New York, 1955

2. Ibid., p. 59

3. Ibid., p. 59

4. Ibid., p. 55 In this chapter, as in the previous chapter, when directly quoting Bonhoeffer, I will use the pronouns which he used, even though I am confident he intended them to be gender generic and inclusive.

5. Matthew 5:17

6. Op. Cit., <u>Ethics</u>, p. 220

7. From the talk, "The Christ of History," first printed in booklet form in the *Image: Journal of the Ecumenical Institute: Chicago*, Number 7, June 1969. The quotation here is from *Bending History,* p. 44, Resurgence Publishing, 2005, John L. Epps, General Editor

8. Op. Cit., p. 248

9. Op. Cit., p. 217

10. Genesis 3:5

11. Op. Cit., p. 220

12. Charles Scribner's Sons, New York, 1967

13. Edited by Edward James Wynne, Jr. And Henry O. Thomson, University Press of America, Inc., Washington D.C., 1982, p. 34

14. Ibid., p. 49

15. Ibid., p. 50-51

16. Ibid., p. 51

17. *Prayer as Ballast, Rudder, and Sail,* OneTree Productions, New Windsor, Maryland, Second Edition, p. 38

Chapter V: Cold Facts about Hot Issues

How our lust for certitude divides the world

James Thurber says somewhere that people can be divided into two groups: There are those who divide people into two groups, and there are those who don't. (A delightfully ironic statement indicting Thurber and all the rest of us who prefer to think we are not among those who divide people into two groups.) In fact, the human tendency toward binary thinking springs eternal, and we continue to come upon ourselves again and again perceiving the world in terms of "them" or "us." Usually, not even our use of the alphabetical categories "A" and "B" opens up the possibilities of "C," "D," etc. Often we speak of "A" and "B" as antithetical to one another instead of options in a series of options.

The proclivity to reduce multiplicity to a more manageable "two" is especially convenient in the realms of politics and religion. At an international level, it allows national leaders to speak of "the evil empire," "the axis of evil," "the great Satan," "you are either for us or against us." At the level of national politics, we are divided into "left or right", "red or blue," "conservative or liberal." And speaking religiously, we are "saved or unsaved," "conservative or progressive," "secular or religious," while interpreting the scripture as "fundamentalists or modernists." As a nation of "twos," one of the great sociological statements of our times is "We don't do nuances."

Such a statement, however, is more than sociological; it is also psychological. It is born of *uncertainty* – one of the most unsettling conditions of the mind and unnerving of the emotions. The only thing worse than living with a known and threatening malady is living with the stress and dread of that malady unnamed, its origin and prognosis unknown. And this is true of uncertainty at almost every level of our lives, including complex and controversial social issues which lend themselves to more than one (or two) interpretations. Such issues usually carry us far beyond the binary luxury of choosing between "A" and "B". Rather, they represent a whole alphabet of choices, and, as indicated in the previous chapter, our problem is not a dearth of options; our problem is an almost overwhelming array of perspectives and "solutions."

One of the easier ways out of this dilemma is to simply deny the multiple options and choose to live in a world where everything is "black and white," "good and bad," "A" and "B". This not only provides one with an escape hatch out of ambivalence and ambiguity, but once a choice is made, it provides a "welcome mat" to condemning and demonizing those who hold a different point of view. In a world of absolutes, you're either "right" or "wrong."

Another exit out of agonizing over controversial issues is to ignore the issues entirely and live in a make-believe world where there is nothing more to life than family, friends and personal issues such as one's health, entertainment, travel and immediate vocational matters. This is the "Shangri-la" in which most Americans live today, and it is refreshingly free of having to ponder health-care reform, environmental policies, debt retirement, and a myriad of other national and international issues – not the least of them being what to do about Iran, Afghanistan, the Taliban and al Qaeda. Planning a trip to Disney World is the more typical American priority.

There is, of course, one further option: to take seriously what Dietrich Bonheoffer meant by "sharing in the life of Christ." This would mean sharing, as Jesus did, in the pain of underprivileged suffering people, victims of social, political and economic devastation. Sharing in such pain is not sitting around, sympathetically wringing one's hands, nor being overwhelmed and paralyzed by the enormity of injustice and suffering in the world. Rather, it is to decide to live according to the best kept secret of the ages: *You give your life in order to find it, and, you engage*

the particular to address the universal. Each of us will live out this paradox
in different ways, not as a "Lone Ranger," but as participating in a community which shares a common discipline and vision, working on behalf
of social justice and making the world more human. And, not incidental-
ly, this is not a decision made "once and for all," rather, it is a decision
made over and over again.

Because complex and controversial issues most often pertain to
human welfare, sharing in Christ's life means participating in those issues, being informed about them, and acting as an advocate for
implementing their solution. Such advocacy should be robust and im-
passioned without presuming to be absolute or to demonize those who
hold a different point of view. Applying Bonhoeffer's radical *freedom* and
radical *obligation* will almost always evoke variations in *responsible* interpretations and decisions. Bonhoeffer insists:

> *It is difficult, or even impossible, to judge from outside whether in a par-
> ticular concrete instance an action is responsible or whether it is
> enthusiastic or legalistic; there are, however, criteria for self-
> examination, though even these cannot afford complete certainty about
> one's own ego.* [1]

What follows in this chapter is my advocacy of four so-called "hot
button" issues. In each instance, I have offered the most compelling case
that I can make, without giving space to other *responsible* positions on that
same issue. However, I should point out that in the References and Notes,
I have noted variations in Bonhoeffer's point of view and mine, and have
briefly stated his conclusion. At the same time, in all four subjects under
consideration, the tension between radical *freedom* and radical *obligation*
has been the context for arriving at the most *responsible* decision I could
make.

Abortion and Measuring the Unmeasurable

The issue of abortion is best considered in relation to the familiar
story of two women who enter the court of King Solomon hoping for the

adjudication of a complex domestic issue, (I Kings 3:16-28) The women have been living in the same house and have born children three days apart. The second woman to give birth rolled over on her child while she slept and killed it. Then, under the cover of darkness, she switched the two infants, placing the dead child at the bosom of the other sleeping mother. When that mother awoke, she recognized that the infant was not her own. She accused the other woman of exchanging babies; the accusation was denied, and a bitter quarrel ensued. In keeping with the custom of the time, the women bring the dispute – and the live child – to Solomon for some kind of resolution.

With no evidence or eye-witnesses except the two women – each claiming to be the mother of the child – Solomon proposes, with apparent seriousness, a biologically literal, legalistic and absurd solution to the dispute. He sends for a sword and announces that he will cleave the child in two, giving half to one woman and half to the other. But before the sword can fall, the real mother urges that the child be given to the other mother – who agrees to settle for the child slain and divided. At that point, Solomon recognizes the woman who is really on the side of the infant's well-being, and awards the child to its true mother.

The point of the story I find most instructive in relation to the abortion issue, is Solomon's wisdom in deciding the issue, not on the basis of a literal calibration – equal parts of a dead infant to each mother – but on the basis of what would serve the health and wholeness of the child, including its well-being in the future. Persons, today, who oppose abortion under any circumstance, base their position on a measurement: They presume to "know" the exact moment when human life begins. This presumption is so absolute as to ignore not only a process that is surely one of the most awesome and complex of any process in the universe, but also ignore the preponderance of medical findings as to how, over time, the process unfolds and creatively manifests itself as human life.

On what basis can we assume to "know," with certitude, the precise instant when a fertilized ovum becomes a person? Is it when a sperm enters an egg, or when, shortly after conception, the zygote or genotype is formed (an entity entirely different from the mother or the father)? Could it be during the first 10 to 14 days when a colony of cells moves through the fallopian tube, dividing and subdividing into a pre-embryo – most of which ends up forming the placenta? Perhaps it is when that colony of cells burrows into the wall of the uterus, and some cells boarding on an inner cavity begin to form an embryo. On the other hand, it might be when a rudimentary heart begins to beat during the 4th week, or when reflex movements are detected at the 6th or 7th weeks. Brain waves are discernable at around 8 weeks, and a neurological capacity for consciousness and pain appears after 26th to 28th weeks. Is one of these moments the tipping-point for calibrating when suddenly we can detect a human being? And what of those Jewish theologians who argue that we are not really dealing with a person until the child is physically separated at birth from the mother?

To be sure, at the time of conception, the correct number of chromosomes is present to form a human life. The genetic code is there. But is that microscopic chemical reaction the equivalent of a human being – as an acorn is the equivalent of an oak tree? What are we discussing here, an isolated point in a chemical reaction which lends itself to a precise calculation? Or, are we reflecting on an extraordinary process which only finds completion through gestation in a protracted period of time?

Such questions bode an uncertainty which many people find unbearable, and so, too often, ecclesiastical bodies step in with dogmas and pronouncements. Thomas Aquinas taught that the soul was given to males on the 40th day after conception and to females on the 80th day, a position held by the Roman Catholic Church until the 13th Century when Pope Innocent III ruled that "ensoulment" or fetal animation occurred approximately four months after conception. It was not until 1869, little more than a hundred years ago, that the Roman Church prohibited abortion at any time and for any reason – not even to save the life of the woman. Over the two thousand years of church history, that's a rather recent position to announce, *ex cathedra*, as the "will of God."

The Roe vs. Wade decision of the U. S. Supreme in 1973 took seriously the creation of human life as *process*, a developmental dynamic which science, for all its innovations, cannot supplant. In a word, the Court allowed for the "unknown." It presumed no certitude as to which moment in gestation was the equivalent of a human being. Consequently it proceeded to offer a trimester format where, according to progression in maturation, certain interests could be served

By applying to Roe vs. Wade the criteria set forth in the previous chapter, it seems apparent that the statute gives priority to the *freedom* of a woman, in consultation with her physician, to determine whether the completion of the pregnancy will be in the best interest of herself and the child. In the latter months of the process, the statute favors the *obligation* to guard the sanctity and right of the fetus, and, in most circumstances, this means bringing the pregnancy to term. Even within these parameters, there are no guarantees that the statute will eliminate occasional abuse. But, by and large, Roe vs. Wade comes about as close as a mature society can come to providing a legal context for making *responsible* decisions about a very personal, dynamic and complex issue.

Homosexuality and Determining Its Cause

According to our best science at the time, the origin of homosexuality, like the inception of a human life, cannot be isolated into a frozen moment to be analyzed and measured. It too is a process. Both heterosexuality and homosexuality are pre-determined by factors which interact over a period of time. While there is some diversity in medical and scientific opinions about the origin of "sexual preference," there is a considerable consensus that any of the possibilities – genetic code variations, hormone distribution, early environmental influences – are all beyond the realm of a person being the instigator of his or her own sex.

This absence of exactitude in determining the origin of sexual preference is more than just lamented by many people; it is construed as threatening. It not only introduces an unwelcome element of doubt into one's moral superiority over being heterosexual, it raises questions about the security of one's own sexuality, and introduces the possibility that being "straight" or "gay" is not a condition one has chosen. This would mean that "sexual preference," rather than being quite literally a "preference," is in reality, a "given" which cannot be reversed, and for which one cannot take credit or be blamed. Thus, the only legitimately moral question which can be asked about this issue is: "What does it mean to be moral *within* the sexuality in which I find myself, the sexuality I know experientially, firsthand?"

In the United States, the most frequent source referred to for condemning homosexuality is the Bible. Even though the words "homosexual" and "heterosexual" are never mentioned in the Bible, it is, nevertheless, a favorite point of reference for fundamentalists and literalists who ignore historical context, and give their own interpretations to Bible verses. One of their favorite scriptures in the Old Testament is the Book of Leviticus – especially Chapters 17 through 26. Those nine chapters constitute what is known as the "Holiness Code." Scholars tell us the code is a compilation of protocols and laws written over several generations sometime in the 6th century, B.C. The purpose of the code was to keep the Israelites' bloodline pure and to protect the Jews against being defiled when they found themselves in a pagan culture – as they did in the land of Canaan, and later when they were exiled in Babylon. Over time, as occasionally happens, those laws became excessive and extreme. This was especially true for that part of the code in Chapter 20 which announces God's demand that adulterers (verse 10), men who lie "with a male as with a woman" (verse 13)," and children who disrespect their parents (verse 9), be stoned to death. The next chapter has God refusing access to the holy altar to "one who is blind or lame, or one who has a mutilated face or a limb too long, or one who has a broken back, or a dwarf, or a man with blemish in his eyes or an itching disease or scabs or crushed testicles." (21:18-20) While the literalist has no choice but to take such injunctions as "God's commands," biblical scholarship and a little common sense tell us we have been reading about the cultural biases and idiosyncrasies of people in a certain century, and not commands that have come down from "on high."

As far as Jesus teachings are concerned, as reported in the Synoptic Gospels, there is no reference directly or indirectly to homosexuality. The only reference that can be found in the New Testament is in the writings of the Apostle Paul. As a citizen of the Greco-Roman world, he knew two kinds of homosexuality – both exploitive and centered in debauchery. One had to do with male masters sexually exploiting male slaves, and the other had to do with the practice of homosexuality among temple prostitutes. Paul condemned them both, as we would. He knew nothing about a homosexuality characterized by mutual consent, genuine affection and monogamous commitment. All of which is to say: One shouldn't "cherry pick" the Bible on this subject without making some effort to become familiar with the cultural and historic circumstances in which the subject is presented.

The key to an informed civility about homosexuality begins with a tolerance for some uncertainty about its origin. For all our medical and scientific knowledge, we simply do not know exactly all the factors which contribute to a person's proclivity for one gender over the other. Most of the evidence thus far indicates the phenomenon is more a process than an instantaneous development. Additionally, we also know that over 40 years ago, the American Medical Association and the American Psychiatric Association announced they do not consider homosexuality to be a mental or emotional disorder, and this information is consistent with the data on pedophilia – the sexual molestation of children. Pedophilia *is* an emotional defect, found almost exclusively in *heterosexual* men – not homosexuals.

From a personal perspective, I have long believed that one of the best "laboratories" for testing the implications of this subject is one's self.

Each of us is expert at knowing what it means to experience sexuality from the inside out. And, within that "laboratory," I cannot recall choosing to be a heterosexual. From adolescence on, being heterosexual was not a choice for me; it was just the way I *felt.* The only choice was, "What does it mean to be ethical and moral within this 'given'"? And, if this has been true for me, could it not also be true for gays and lesbians? If they have experienced their sexuality as I have, how unfair, if not disgraceful has been the church's condescending insistence that the only moral option for gays and lesbians is celibacy, refraining from any expression of their sexuality. Rather than such a double standard, why not define morality for gays and straights in terms of mutual consent, genuine affection and monogamous commitment (standards which would require my own denomination to rethink its prohibition against performing marriages for same-sex couples)?

I should add that probably the surest way into a new perspective on this issue is to make a friend of someone who is homosexual. What you'll discover is a person who no more wants to be exhaustively defined by his or her sexuality than you or I do. All of us are sexual beings, and yet as powerful as is that dynamic, there is so much more to us than sexuality. We are people with a huge repertoire of fears and tears, hopes and dreams, joys and sorrows, and in every one of us there is a deep-down longing to be treated with dignity and respect. There is no place in our society where an inclusive "welcome" is more clearly mandated than in a community of faith. The first place one would think to look for such an affirmation of dignity and respect would be the church, or else what did the author of the Gospel of Luke have in mind when he had Jesus tell a parable about a banquet which concludes with the master saying "all are welcome at this table."? (Luke 14:12-24)

By viewing this issue through the lens of Bonhoeffer's *freedom* and *obligation*, it becomes apparent that, on the one hand, an immature Christianity exchanges the *freedom* of rational inquiry for an offering of certitude from Biblical literalism, arbitrary church pronouncements, or a moral superiority inferred by presuming sexuality to be a "choice." On the other hand, a Christianity come-of-age will not only embrace the *freedom* to think critically about this subject, but will also honor the *obligation* to take seriously knowledge represented by the aforementioned scholarly and professional disciplines, as well as insights transmitted through historic wisdom and traditions. It is in this tension between *freedom* and *obligation* that 21st Century Christians forge *responsible* decisions about homosexuality.

Gun Laws and Their Opposition

The almost knee-jerk opposition to gun legislation in America today is due primarily to three great uncertainties. In the first place, among many people there is the uncertainty of not knowing if or when they will be victims of a domestic crime. And this unsettling awareness is made all the more intense by a lack of trust in local law enforcement to provide protection. Therefore, the perceived "solution" to such vulnerability is a firearm in every home, despite the fact that 80% of persons killed by handguns are shot, not by outlaws, but by in-laws, relatives, and various family members. The victims know each other, love each other; they are wives and husbands, parents and children, brothers and sisters who intentionally or accidentally take each other's lives. One of the serious proposals to the classroom killings of students at Virginia Tech in 2007 was a recommendation to arm the student body. Such irrational propositions seem rational only when persons are so desperately anxious about their safety that they will cling to the most unlikely odds that by acquiring a gun they will make themselves and their families safer.

In the second place, among a segment of the population, there exists a paranoia and fear that government and the military cannot protect us from external threats. This anxiety is seldom expressed directly, but surfaces, more times than not by invoking Article II in the Bill of Rights of the U. S. Constitution: "A well regulated Militia, being necessary to the security of a Free State, the right of the people to keep and bear Arms shall not be infringed." The historical context motivating the framers of the Constitution to proclaim this freedom was the practice of monarchs to disarm their subjects for the purpose of controlling them. Of course the colonists, fighting for a Democracy, were by force of early circumstances bearers of arms.

As the reader is doubtlessly aware, the interpretation of this amendment has been tested in the Courts time and again, especially the intent of the amendment's reference to the right of states to maintain "well regulated militias." The National Rifle Association has insisted for decades that the amendment should be interpreted as a carte blanche entitlement for citizens to arm themselves. In 1982, the U. S. Supreme Court let stand the ruling of the 7th Circuit Court reading, "It is clear that the right to bear arms is inextricably connected to the preservation of the militia. The right to keep and bear handguns is not guaranteed by the second amendment." Consistent with that ruling was the ruling of the Court in January of 1991, with the NRA challenging the right of Congress to ban the manufacture of machine guns intended for sale to private citizens, the Supreme Court let stand a lower court ruling defeating the NRA opposition.

One can only speculate as to why citizens of this democracy feel the need to be in possession of machine guns, assault weapons and Teflon coated ammunition that penetrate bullet-proof vests, but such a "need" at least appears to imply a sense of deep insecurity and a lack of confidence in one's own government. On the other hand, among my friends who enjoy hunting, skeet shooting and contests at target ranges, not one of them opposes gun registration or a waiting period for background checks into criminality, mental illness, etc. The organization most consistently against such safe guards is the Nation Rifle Association.

The third possible explanation for a preoccupation with weaponry is even more cynical and paranoid than the others; it is the belief that citizens must arm themselves against their own government lest the United States use federal troops against the population. Like those who believe they must personally arm themselves to repel a foreign enemy, this third position is seldom overt or direct about its motivation; it too appeals to the Second Amendment for its justification. And, for obvious reasons, it is quick to find common cause with other groups and organizations opposing gun legislation.

A fear of the "unknown" seems to characterize all of these endeavors, causing some to distrust law enforcement, and others to doubt the efficacy of a constitutionally provided military. What they have in common is a willingness to ignore the odds that the more they arm themselves; the more they increase the danger to both themselves and others. By making a Constitutional *freedom* an absolute, *responsible* safeguards are denied, and an *obligation* for the common good is lost. Gun-related accidents, criminal exploitation and indiscriminate killings proliferate, and America continues to lead the world with more violent deaths per capita, by far, than any other nation.

War: Pacifist, "Just War Doctrine" or "Shock and Awe"?

Of the four issues considered in this chapter, I find the moral and ethical implications of war the most vexing and ambiguous. Consequently, it is the issue about which I am the most ambivalent. Through the years, the road I have been traveling in relation to this subject has taken me from being a non-pacifist to becoming a near-pacifist, and I am still traveling on the journey. Or, at the moment, as a friend of mine has put it, "I'm a non-pacifist in recovery." It is for this reason that I have decided to present the issue in the more personal context of my own struggle.

One of my guides along the way has been the theologian, Reinhold Niebuhr. I have learned much from him, even though he made his journey through this issue at a different time in history, resulting in each of us having traveled from opposite directions to opposite destinations. Niebuhr, as a young pastor, held a pacifist position, and eventually served as the national chairman of the Fellowship of Reconciliation. However, even at that time, his pacifist sympathies were practical and pragmatic. He knew that pacifists could only achieve their goal when those they resisted were potential allies, ethical and conscientious, as with the case of Gandhi's struggle against the British. Furthermore, he was always clear about his own complicity in sin, and that his choice of pacifist philosophy was relative at best.

By 1932, Niebuhr had left the pacifist position, becoming more and more alarmed by the relentless aggression of Adolph Hitler and the futility of European appeasement. Just before World War II, he was instrumental in founding the periodical, "Christianity and Crisis," in order to counteract a pacifist trend in churches. War, he believed, horrible as it may be, is preferable to surrendering to a totalitarian system.

By the time I had classes with him at Union Theological Seminary, he considered absolute pacifism to be a "very sentimentalized" form of the Christian faith. He argued that the Reformation doctrine of "Justification by Faith" doesn't offer a grace that lifts human beings out of "the sinful contradictions of history," but rather empowers them to confess their sin and be forgiven, while knowing that there is no way to live in history without sinning. Such an assumption does not exempt Christians from being as ethical and moral as possible, but it does deliver them from the pretension of a superior righteousness. Niebuhr was as hard on non-pacifist as pacifists.

At the same time, however, for all of his support for World War II, he never demeaned the pacifist position, and in 1940 he wrote:

> *We who allow ourselves to become engaged in war, need the testimony of the absolutist against us, lest we accept the warfare of the world as normative, lest we become callous to the horror of war, and lest we forget the ambiguity of our own actions and motives and the risk we run of achieving no permanent good from the momentary anarchy in which we are involved.* [4]

Like Niebuhr, I have always considered the defeat of Nazi aggression and its "final solution to the Jewish problem" to be about as close as we could come to a "good war," notwithstanding my conviction that the dropping of the atomic bomb was heinously unjustified. And, for most of my ministry, I have been an advocate for measuring violent conflict by criteria set forth in the "Just War Doctrine." In brief, this a doctrine propounded by Augustine in the 4th Century when Christian teaching challenged any resort to violence. While Augustine opposed wars of aggression and aggrandizement, he further believed that there were times when resorting to force may be tragically required – never a normative good, but a tragic necessity. Through the centuries, there emerged the concept of the "just war" as the lesser of two evils, and always defined by principles of last resort, proportionality, prudent expectation, and the immunity of noncombatants from direct attack. This has meant that, on occasions, Christians like Dietrich Bonhoeffer, with a strong presumption for peace and non-violence, have decided to "sin bravely" for the greater good.

By now, I have no doubt the reader has discovered I am less than enthusiastic about the administration of George W. Bush, and I continue to question the U. S. Supreme Court's unprecedented intervention in the Florida electoral process by which he was "awarded" the presidency. Later, I blanched every time he naively repeated the jihad, holy war rhetoric of the other side, referring to them – as they referred to us – as "evil." Nevertheless, despite all these reservations, on September 11, 2001, following Al Qaeda's unprovoked attack on the U. S, and the killing of several thousand of our citizens, I supported the President's decision to declare war against the Taliban – Al Qaeda's host in Afghanistan. As I indicated in an earlier chapter, that decision was widely supported at the time by both the American people and the international community. It was strictly a defensive measure, and not the equivalent of America's later "peremptory" invasion of Iraq. The deceptions launching that invasion will always blight it as unnecessary and enormously tragic.

All of the above then has led me to reconsider the implications of warfare in the 21st Century – even when it's "justified" by an appeal to principles of the "Just War Doctrine." How much in that Doctrine is really left after the "proportionate," the "prudent" or the "protection of noncombatants" have been shredded by megaton bombs, remotely guided drones and missiles, and other state-of-the-art hardware for killing? Despite all of our best efforts to be selective of targets, the "collateral damage" now standard parlance in modern warfare continues to take a horrific toll of women, children and other innocents.

War is no longer the squaring off of two enemies on a battle field; it has become the indiscriminate destruction of human beings *en mass.* "Just war" and "smart bombs" may be the two great oxymorons of the modern world, and, as with the atomic bombs of Hiroshima and Nagasaki, our capacity to kill may have at last exceeded all rationalizations for the use of violence. It's beginning to look like we have no choice but to radically reconsider how we're going to live together.

But what does such a consideration really look like and require of each of us as we struggle with the paradoxical *obligation* to protect the innocent from unprovoked aggression on the one hand, while on the other hand, to live not only in peace with others but to risk ourselves and put our lives on the line for peace as well? Such imperatives are made all the more excruciating by coming to us in the context of a radical *freedom* where there are no sure answers. And so we wear this "shirt of flame," knowing that not even our most *responsible* decision can be exonerating or leave us feeling righteous.

These are some of the reflective steps that I've been taking in an attempt to be in both the 21st Century *and* in Jesus Christ. They are faltering steps at best, even though I like to think that, were Reinhold Niebuhr living at this time in history, he might, himself, entertain some of these same reflections. What I am almost sure of is that, whatever his conclusions, my old mentor would continue to insist that "sin is inevitable but not necessary," and that the ultimate hope for all of us, pacifist and non-pacifist alike, is in the unconditional grace of God. (5)

Notes and References

1. *Ethics,* The Macmillan Company, New York, 1955, p.226.

2. In all fairness to Bonhoeffer, I cannot claim that his arrival at a *responsible* decision on the subject of abortion is the same as mine. On the contrary, he believed that even a *potentially* human life was the will of God, and should not be aborted. However, he also favored the principle of birth control when a particular instance called for the limitation of the number of children. And, this position, today, would be in conflict with the most common forms of birth control – IUDs and low-dose birth control pills. Correctly labeled by the medical community as "abortifacients," these devices and medication cause an abortion soon after the fertilization of an egg. Furthermore, there is no way to know with certainty what Bonhoeffer's position would be on this subject were he living almost seven decades later in a society presuming the right of a women to continue or discontinue her pregnancy in its early stages, and the right of a fetus to be brought to term in the later stages. *Ethics,* The Macmillan Company, 1955, p. 130-132.

3. Scholars generally agree that while the poor, the crippled, the lame, and the blind were objects of Jesus' compassion, in this particular dinner party parable, Luke is here expressing himself rather than reporting what Jesus said. *The Five Gospels*, New Translation and Commentary by Robert W. Funk, Roy W. Hoover, and the Jesus Seminar, Harpers, San Francisco, 1997, p. 351.

4. Quoted by E. J. Dionne, Jr., "Pacifists, Serious and Otherwise," *Washington Post*, October 21, 2001

5. Bonhoeffer, writing at the time of World War II, draws a clear distinction between pre-Christian wars and "western wars." He writes

> *So long as there are to be western wars they cannot, therefore ever be total wars. Total war makes use of all conceivable means which may possibly serve the purpose of national self-preservation. Anything which*

> *is of advantage to one's own cause is rightful and permissible. ... the enemy, whether he be armed or defenseless, is treated as a criminal.* (Op. Cit., p. 30)

One can't help but wonder what Bonhoeffer would say today about the atomic bomb, the nuclear bomb, and even more recent weapons of indiscriminate, mass destruction.

Chapter VI: Redefining "Mental Health"

Embracing Vulnerability and Existential Anxiety

For the mature Christian, leaving childish ways behind not only means taking responsibility for one's life through decision-making, it also means living in a real world of risks and dangers. No longer able to count on providential interventions or traditional "divine guidance," we have no choice but to be vulnerable to a variety of threats to our well-being. Acknowledging this vulnerability and the emotions it occasions is crucial to understanding what it means to be both genuinely human *and* a mature Christian in the 21st Century.

Such acknowledgment, however, is especially difficult to come by in our society since so much of the prevailing culture is based on denying vulnerability and avoiding facing deep, unsettling emotions. Too often, "mental health" is defined as the absence of such emotions. A "normal person" is represented as well-adjusted, mastering life's exigencies and having at least the appearance of being unperturbed and "in control." The secular world rewards such "normalcy" in a variety of ways, while the religious world reinforces it with spiritual formulas for "peace of mind," and various rescue strategies that promise a "way out" of anxiety-producing predicaments.

But what if mental health, in a mature Christianity, is just the opposite? What if being in Jesus Christ means acknowledging our vulnerability as finite creatures, taking seriously the threats to our existence, and finding ways to live meaningfully without being paralyzed by risks and dangers? This would suggest that much of the abnormality we call "mental illness" has its origin, not in the presence of psychic anxieties, but in our unwillingness or inability to come to terms with them. What if the well-kept secret of the Christian faith is that we can look deep into the threats to our existence, honestly "own" the emotions they occasion, and embrace our vulnerability in generative and creative ways?

Paul Tillich

There is considerable consensus among scholars in both the disciplines of theology and psychology that no one explored the interfacing of theology and psychoanalysis with greater insight than Paul Tillich. He made it possible for countless modern men and women to become or remain Christian without ceasing to be modern men and women. From 1933 to 1955, he was Professor of Philosophical Theology at New York's Union Theological Seminary, while also serving on the faculty in Columbia's Department of Psychology. He was the only person to ever hold the two chairs concurrently. Tillich believed it was impossible to elaborate on a Christian doctrine of what it means to be human, without using the immense material brought forth by the disciplines of depth-psychology. Rollo May, one of his students, who went on to become a renowned psychoanalyst, referred to him as "the analyst's analyst."

Tillich's classic work in combining theology and depth-psychology is *The Courage To Be*. [1] Just as Dietrich Bonhoeffer provided vanguard insights into Christian ethics for a modern world, so Paul Tillich broke new ground in exploring theological implications for the human psyche. For the remainder of this chapter, we will consider his analysis of what he called "existential anxieties," and in the next chapter we will look at his use of "courage" as the fundamental premise for approaching those anxieties through faith.

First, I would like to offer a word about the origin of Tillich's method of doing theology. It was not abstract or esoteric. Like Bonhoeffer, he grounded theological interpretations in the specific and experiential. His method came into being while he served as a chaplain in World War I. During a battle on the Marne, his fellow officers were brought in on stretchers, chopped to pieces by gunfire, wounded or dead. That night "absolutely transformed me," he would say. "All my friends were among those dying and dead. That night I became an existentialist." [2]

The word "existentialism" is often used as a reference to philosophies associated with Jean-Paul Sartre, Martin Heidegger and Friedrich Nietzsche. It is found in various literary works by Albert Camus, Fyodor Dostoevsky and Franz Kafka. In Christian history, its influence is evident in the writings of Soren Kierkegaard, Martin Luther, St. Augustine, and some would say, in the Apostle Paul. It is further claimed that one of the earliest existentialists was Socrates.

As to the meaning of the word, one of the most accurately succinct definitions I have come across is given by Robert Solomon, Professor of Philosophy at the University of Texas. He says, "In a word: Existentialism is the philosophy of No Excuses." [3] That is to say, we are responsible for ourselves, and for delving deeply into what it means to be a human being.   As adults, without supernatural props to keep us from being vulnerable, we were meant to explore the ultimate meaning of our existence in all its finitude and limitations. No excuses.

Paul Tillich became an existentialist theologian that night on the battlefield when he decided that unless theology takes responsibility for connecting us to the primal issues of our existence, it is irrelevant. Talk about God that is "academic" and abstract is useless. Tillich is interested only in questions that are asked out of the very depths of being, questions forged in the "life juices" of absolute concerns. Such questions as, "Why am I here?" "Where am I going?" "How will I meet my death?" "What is the meaning of this brief stretch between womb and tomb?" Address these questions in the name of Jesus Christ, or keep mercifully silent. No excuses. "I seek to explain the contents of the Christian faith through existential questions and theological answers in mutual interdependence." said Tillich. This "method of correlation" is the Hallmark of his work, and *The Courage To Be* is his premier attempt to show such a correlation between the manifestations of anxiety in the human psyche and the Word in Jesus Christ.

Being and Nonbeing

Admittedly, at first glance, the words *being* and *nonbeing* appear terribly esoteric, the very essence of abstraction. However, Tillich uses them to imply a meaning that is inescapably common and specific. *Being* is simply existence. To have being is to be, to exist, to have a life, to participate in the process of becoming. Your consciousness, your unconsciousness, your birth, relationships, solitude, longevity, aging, last breath – all that constitutes your identity and the "going-on-ness" of your life – is what Tillich calls your being.

Nonbeing is the logical opposite of *being*. It is to have no existence, even though our awareness of its inevitability is a part of being. Each of us knows that there was a time when we were not, a time before our birth when we had no being. This time occurred in our absence, and human history unfolded without our presence.

Furthermore, we sense that there will be a time once again when we will have no being, a time when other lives survive us and history unfolds once more without us. Nonbeing is the negative side of being; every creature comes out of it and returns.

The above definitions of *being* and *nonbeing* are not just intellectual propositions. They are realities present in "the marrow of our bones," and are the source of a profoundly troubling emotion. That emotion is what Tillich calls "existential anxiety," the state of being aware of both one's being, and the inevitable prelude and postlude of nonbeing. To say that this anxiety is "existential," is to say "it is wired" into the human psyche at the level of deep emotions we cannot escape. Later we will see that acknowledging this anxiety is the prerequisite to living a courageous and authentic life.

The Anxiety of Fate and Death

Tillich distinguishes three types of existential anxiety according to the three ways in which nonbeing threatens being. He is careful to point out that these types are inherent in our existence; they belong to being and "not to an abnormal state of mind as in neurotic (and psychotic) anxiety." [4] Put plainly, these types of anxiety are found in every person, including the most "normal," and they are commensurate with the most positive definitions of "mental health." Furthermore, difference in types does not mean mutual exclusion. Each of the types is imminent in each other, but normally under the dominance of one of them.

The first is an existential anxiety about fate and ultimately about death. The term, "fate" refers to the unpredictable, capricious nature of our existence. It is fate's randomness that can reduce a proud and resolute man or woman to helplessness and despair. It is what prompts soldiers to speculate on what it would have been like if a bullet had been a half an inch higher or three quarters of an inch to the right? It is found in the enigma of what causes car A to collide with car B instead of car C or D; what causes a virus to strike one child and not another; what causes one person to be born at a certain place and time to certain parents, while another person is born into an altogether different set of circumstances? These "accidents of history" constitute a "fate" outside of our control.

The same is true for the opaqueness of the future. Enigmatic and unpredictable, tomorrow and the day after are, at best, a matter of speculation. The only thing we know with certainty about the future is that we do not know with certainty about the future. The modern artist, Georgio de Chirico, has a painting of a little girl, carefree and skipping along a lighted street at night. She is approaching a dark corner, and around that corner is a shadow which reaches ominously toward her. She is moving, as we all are, toward what Tillich calls "the irrationality, the impenetrable darkness of fate." [5]

What sustains our anxiety about fate and gives it its power is death. Death is so basic, so inescapable and universal, that at the deepest level of our being nothing can dissuade us of its reality:

All attempts to argue it away are futile. Even if the so-called arguments for the 'immortality of the soul' had argumentative power (which they do not have) they would not convince existentially. For existentially every-body is aware of the complete loss of self which biological extinction implies. (6)

This power of death is not limited to just that last moment when we move from being to nonbeing; it stands behind all our vulnerabilities and exigencies. The inevitability of death insinuates itself into every ill-ness, every loss, every accident and weakness. Feeling tired in the evening, not having enough time to complete a project, never knowing as much as we want to know or need to know about a subject, acquiring grey hair and wrinkles, the death of a friend or loved one – everywhere we turn there are reminders that we are in the process of dying, and the anxiety of nonbeing is ever present.

> *We try to transform this anxiety into fear and to meet courageously the objects in which the threat is embodied. We succeed partly, but somehow we are aware of the fact that it is not these objects with which we strug-gle that produce the anxiety but the human situation as such.* (7)

It is this "human situation as such," this primal threat to our exis-tence that becomes the context for the question: "Is there a courage to affirm oneself in spite of a threat to one's deepest self-affirmation?"

The Anxiety of Emptiness and Meaninglessness
The second form of anxiety produced by the threat of nonbeing is the anxiety of emptiness, which has behind it the awfulness of meanin-glessness.

Each of us experiences moments of significance and purpose. In such moments we love ourselves and what comes into being through us. Living creatively is not just being creative in the sense that the artist or the genius is creative; it is living spontaneously with the contents of one's cultural life. It is entering fully into family, vocation, society, nature, the arts, etc. To love all these things is to love them because they actualize our own fulfillment, and because their fulfillment is actualized through us. By our participation in them, we change them and are changed by them.

On the other hand, we know what it means to experience emptiness and a loss of purpose – hours that hang heavy, periods of monotony, moments of boredom. Meaningful experiences cannot be frozen; they come into being and move inexorably toward nonbeing. We take delight in having arrived at an intellectual understanding of a difficult problem, only to discover later that the same problem is once again opaque to us. We have rapport with another human being and are able to communicate with remarkable clarity, only to find on another occasion with that same person, we are "talking past" each other. The never-ceasing and never-satisfied sexual libido appears, disappears, reappears, and is never permanently at rest. Sounds of music send the spirit soaring, works of art inspire, delicious foods delight the pallet, but nothing endures.

In the background of emptiness lies meaninglessness as death lies in the background of fate. Transitory and ephemeral meanings cause us to wonder about the permanence of any meaning. Being driven from one passion and devotion to another, each with a meaning that eventually slips away, can lead finally to indifference or aversion. Then, we are in danger of a profound revulsion with everything, for what is lost with meaninglessness is ultimate concern – the meaning which gives meaning to all meanings.

> *Everything is tried and nothing satisfies. ...The anxiety of emptiness drives us to the abyss of meaninglessness.* (8)

From the edge of this abyss, Tillich says a person can try one last way out. There is always the option of turning oneself over to some absolute, spiritual authority of which no further questions can be asked and from which answers are given and certainties imposed. The security in this authority is the guarantee of meaning, which relieves the self of the anxiety of emptiness. But what the self has given up in the trade off is its right to ask and doubt. Freedom is sacrificed to escape meaninglessness, and meaning is saved while the self is lost. (It is, as we described in previous chapters, a regression back to "childishness.")

The clue to the loss of the self is fanatical self-assertiveness:

Fanaticism is the correlate to spiritual self-surrender; it shows the anxiety which it was supposed to conquer, by attacking with disproportionate violence those who disagree and who demonstrate by their disagreement elements in the spiritual life of the fanatic which he must suppress in himself. Because he must suppress them in himself he must suppress them in others. His anxiety forces him to persecute dissenters. The weakness of the fanatic is that those whom he fights have a secret hold upon him; and to this weakness he and his group finally succumb. (9)

This weakness has its origin in the same existential anxiety over the loss of meaning that pervades every other human being, and that causes us to ask: "Is there a courage to *be*, a courage to affirm one's self in spite of emptiness and loss of meaning?"

The Anxiety of Guilt and Condemnation

The anxiety of nonbeing threatens us from a third side; it threatens our moral self-affirmation.

Each of us has a judge within requiring an answer to the question: "What have you made of yourself?" The question demands an answer, and its implication is that there is a certain destiny we are expected to fulfill. We make decisions that are acts of moral self-affirmation and that contribute to the actualization of our potential, even as on other occasions we act against our essential being and lose touch with our sense of destiny. Tillich does not expound in detail on what he means by our "destiny," but it is my sense that he's referring to the capacity in each of us to know when we are making decisions which enhance our own humanity and the humanity of others, and when we are making decisions which betray that humanity in both ourselves and others.

Nikos Kazantzakis has proposed that the destiny which resides in each of us has public implications as well as personal ones, implications which touch both our ancestors and our unborn descendants:

> *As soon as you were born, a new possibility was born with you, a free heartbeat stormed through the great sunless heart of your race.*
>
> *Whether you would or not, you brought a new rhythm, a new desire, a new idea, a fresh sorrow.*
>
> *Whether you would or not, you enriched your ancestral body.*
>
> *Where are you going? How shall you confront life and death, virtue and fear?*
>
> *All the race takes refuge in your breast; it asks questions there, and lies waiting in agony.*
>
> *You have a great responsibility. You do not govern now only your own small, insignificant existence. You are a throw of the dice on which, for a moment, the entire fate of your race is gambled.*
>
> *Everything you do reverberates throughout a thousand destinies. As you walk, you cut open and create that river bed into which the stream of your descendants shall enter and flow.*
>
> *When you shake with fear, your terror branches out into innumerable generations, and you degrade innumerable souls before and behind you. When you rise to a valorous deed, all of your race rises with you and turns valorous.* (10)

To avoid self-rejection and the feeling of being condemned, we attempt to transform the anxiety of guilt into action, an action often flawed and desperate. This can happen in one of two ways. One way is to defy conventional morality, answering to no codes or commandments, and appearing almost driven to affirm the self in opposition to any other person's standards. This is the way of the libertine. The second option is to make an absolute of moral rigor, adopting certain legalisms, and exulting in a moral superiority over others. This is the way of the crusader and self-appointed avenger. However, in each of these instances, the anxiety of guilt lies in the background, and again the question is raised: "Is there a courage to *be*, a courage that can affirm the self in spite of guilt and fear of condemnation?"

Despair and Healing

The pain produced by the three existential anxieties is despair – despair inherent in the very nature of human existence. A person is aware of failing to affirm him or herself because of the irresistible power of non-being, and yet enough being is left to feel both the power of the negation and the futility of being rid of it. Such despair replicates itself, and a person despairs over the pervasiveness of despair.

This despair is a "boundary-line" situation which one cannot go beyond. It is to be without hope where no way out into the future appears. Not even suicide liberates us from the anxiety of guilt and condemnation. While ending one's life can end a stream of consciousness infused with pain, the guilt one feels before the act of suicide anticipates the pain of those who will mourn the death, and thus carries its own inherent condemnation. Tillich concludes, "In view of this character of despair it is understandable that all human life can be interpreted as a continuous attempt to avoid despair." [11]

While each of the three existential anxieties is implicit in the threat of nonbeing, Tillich argues that one of them is bound to be more prevalent than others – depending on the period of history. At the end of ancient civilization and its various conflicts of imperial powers, the anxiety of fate and death was in ascendancy. Individuals quaked at being in the hands of powers, natural and political, which were completely beyond their control and calculation.

The impact of the Jewish-Christian message so changed the situation that toward the end of the Middle Ages the anxiety of guilt and condemnation became decisive. The pre-Reformation and Reformation era was symbolized by the "wrath of God," and people were driven by images of hell and purgatory to various means of assuaging anxiety through pilgrimages, asceticism, devotion to relics, a desire for indulgences, masses, penances and alms – all motivated by the question: "How can I appease the wrath of God?"

The third main period of anxiety appeared with the enlightenment and the development of liberalism, democracy and the rise of a technical civilization. These major changes in the way we understand the world so accelerated the anxiety of emptiness and meaninglessness that it dominates today as the controlling existential threat. Although, to be sure, the other threats are also present.

I will not attempt a detailed discussion of Tillich's analysis of pathological anxiety. While he sees neurosis as an expression of the courage to take the anxiety of nonbeing into itself, as opposed to the extreme alternative of despair, he also sees it as only a partial affirmation of the self. The neurotic, unable to affirm himself or herself in some existential anxieties, is often more sensitive to the presence of these aspects of nonbeing than the average person. Indeed, for this very reason, neurotic people often excel in creativity and are able to give artistic expression to existential threats. Tillich would agree with the observation of Otto Rank that:

> *The more a person is normal, healthy and happy, the more he or she can successfully repress, displace, deny, rationalize and deceive others. So it follows that the suffering of a neurotic comes from painful truth. He or she sees through the deceptions of the world, the falsity of reality. He or she suffers, not from the pathological mechanisms of psychosis, but from the absence of escape mechanisms employed by the great majority of people. It is from being closer to the truth that he or she suffers.* (12)

On the other hand, the psychotic state is indicative of nonbeing's complete triumph over being. Unable to affirm any portion of the self that is experiencing existential anxieties, a person withdraws completely from reality and finds affirmation in a world of illusion. Within this world, the psychotic is secure and well adjusted.

Since psychotic anxieties are exceptional, abnormal conditions, while existential anxieties are a normal, inescapable part of every person's being, a different approach to healing is required for each of them. Tillich states, "Pathological anxiety, once established, is an object of medical healing. Existential anxiety is an object of priestly help." [13] The following chapter explores the latter in relation to Tillich's concept of courage and the "God above God."

Notes and References

1. Yale University Press, New Haven, Conn., 1952

2. Rollo May, *Paulis,* Harper & Row, New York, Evanston, San Francisco, London, 1973, p. 18

3. Robert Solomon, The Great Courses, "No Excuses: Existentialism and the Meaning of Life", The Guide Book, 2000, p.1

4. *The Courage To Be,* Op. Cit., p. 41

5. Ibid., p. 45

6. Ibid., p. 42

7. Ibid., p. 45

8. Ibid., p. 48

9. Ibid., p. 49-51; This quotation stands today as a penetrating analysis of the psychology behind biblical literalism and theological fundamentalism. Rigid orthodoxies and other manifestations of authoritative religion continue to offer the certainties and protections reminiscent of what children require of parents, and that we rightly associate with being less than mature.

10.   Nikos Kazantzakis, *The Saviors of God: Spiritual Exercises,* Translated by Kimon Friar, Simon and Schuster, New York, 1960, p. 72. Tillich would insist, however, that even in our noblest and most "valorous deed," *non-being* is present. It insinuates itself into every self-affirmation, and has the power to drive us into self-contempt.

11. Ibid., p. 56

12. Personal papers of William A. Holmes; Source not known

13. Ibid., p. 77

Chapter VII: Courage and the "God above God"

Living as a 21st Century Person of Faith

> *Courage is self-affirmation "in spite of," that is in spite of that which tends to prevent the self from affirming itself.* [1]

For Paul Tillich, courage is essential to experiencing the meaning of human existence; it is the key to being itself. The good life is the courageous life, the noble and triumphant life. The greater the courage to face normal anxieties, the stronger the self. With approval, Tillich quotes from Nietzche:

> *He hath heart who knoweth fear but* vanquisheth *it; who seeth the abyss, but with* pride. *He who seeth the abyss but with eagle's eyes, - he who with eagle's talons* graspeth *the abyss: he hath courage.* [2]

Courage – coming from the Latin *cor* and the French *coeur*, meaning heart – is not just one virtue among others, but the very premise and bedrock upon which all other virtues depend. It is at the center of our being, and its source is the *"ground of being,"* which is Tillich's way of saying it has its source in God.

For come-of-age Christians, this courage constitutes a deliberate decision to live without seeking exemptions from life's capriciousness, or the existential anxiety such capriciousness bestows. It is a courage made in the full awareness that life is unpredictable, the future is unforeseen, and the only way to maximize the full promise of life's offerings is to decide to live "in spite of."

Courage, like politics, is always local. No one wakes up in the morning feeling abstractly courageous. Courageous decisions and actions exist only in a field of countervailing forces, a context of polarity and tension. The man who puts his job at risk for the sake of certain principles, the woman who jeopardizes a long-standing relationship by confronting the addiction of a friend or family member, the student who passes up an opportunity to cheat on an exam, the first-responder who climbs the stairs of a burning building to save another's life – these and other acts of courage occur only in the context of deciding to forgo certain comfort zones, to challenge certain fears.

When it comes to future terrorists' attacks and an obsessive shrinking of one's life to fit precautionary measures, Senator John McCain throws out one of his plainspoken antidotes to paralyzing fears:

> *Get on the damn elevator! Fly on the damn plane! Calculate the odds of being harmed by a terrorist! It's still about as likely as being swept out to sea by a tidal wave. Suck it up, for crying out loud. You're almost certainly going to be okay. And in the unlikely event you're not, do you really want to spend your last days cowering behind plastic sheets and duct tape? That's not a life worth living, is it?* [3]

During the period of extreme violence between Israelis and Palestinians in the 1990's, when both sides were almost daily employing desperate acts of terror against each other, a bomb killed two dozen young people at a Tel Aviv disco. Israeli youth refused to be cowed, and soon resumed their robust nightlife. Today, outside the scene of the bombing, beneath a stone memorial listing the names of the dead is a single inscription: "*Lo Nafseek Lirkod.*" It means, "We won't stop dancing." [4]

Facing Death

Tillich insists that courage is the imperative required of all persons who face the inevitability of their own deaths – including Christians. He laments that the popular belief in immortality has largely replaced the Christian symbol of resurrection and eternal life. [5] "The immortality of the soul" is a Greek concept that seeks to avoid the anxiety of death by having the soul automatically survive finiteness and continue on as before. This is a cheap solution, since it removes any reason to be anxious about death in the first place. After all, if we don't really die, but simply pass from one sphere to another, what possible need could we have for courage? In fact, who needs the resurrection?

What makes our anxiety about death an existential anxiety is a deep-down, ubiquitous awareness that just as we came into being out of nonbeing, so it is to nonbeing we shall eventually return. It is the fateful reality that when you are dead you are dead, and there is no automatic extension of yourself. Facing that reality takes courage.

For Tillich, and for other Christians, this view of death need not diminish the power of a resurrection faith which entrusts to God the final disposition of the self. It is not a guarantee that a person's stream of self-consciousness will go on *ad infinitum,* nor is it an assurance that any other specific form of being, as we know it, will survive. Martin Luther suggested we can know as much about life beyond death as a fetus traveling down the birth canal about to be born can know about the world it is about to enter. In the full presence of existential anxiousness about nonbeing, the Christian courageously embraces the resurrection as the decision to commend ultimately her or his death to God. Thereby, deciding to trust the ground of being with being itself, and whatever comes after it.

> *For encountering God means encountering transcendent security and transcendent eternity. He who participates in God participates in eternity.* (6)

Guilt and Condemnation

Such courage also makes it possible to live with the vulnerability of anxiety about guilt and condemnation. It is the courage to accept acceptance in spite of the consciousness of guilt. For Tillich, "It is rooted in the personal, total, and immediate certainty of divine forgiveness." (7) It is the Pauline doctrine of "justification by faith," independent of any moral, intellectual or religious preconditions. This is not a self-affirmation that results from being good, or wise or pious. The only persons who plumb the deepest meaning of acceptance are those who know they are unacceptable to themselves and others, and yet have the courage to act as acceptable to God. This is not the philosopher's stoical perseverance, "come what may." Rather, it is the paradoxical act of accepting oneself as accepted while not feeling acceptable.

Tillich's sermons are their own best presentation of this remarkable possibility and promise. Here are two excerpts:

> *Nothing is demanded of you - no idea of God, and no goodness in yourselves, not your being religious, not your being Christian, not your being wise, and not your being moral. But what is demanded is only your being open and willing to accept what is given to you, the New Being .* (8)

> *You are accepted, accepted by that which is greater than you, and the name of which you do not know. Do not ask for the name now; perhaps you will find it later. Do not try to do anything now; perhaps later you will do much. Do not seek for anything; do not perform anything, do not intend anything. Simply accept the fact that you are accepted! ... After such an experience we may not be better than before, and we may not believe more than before. But everything is transformed. In that moment, grace conquers sin, and reconciliation bridges the gulf of estrangement.* (9)

Courage is the operative word when it comes to dealing with guilt. Whether you feel forgiven is not the issue. All that matters is your decision to receive the gift of forgiveness as the ultimate truth about your life – regardless of your feelings. Acting on that truth means deciding to live as a forgiven person, and that takes courage.

Doubt and Meaninglessness

The third type of existential anxiety which courage overcomes is the doubt and meaninglessness so characteristic of the period in which we live. It is the fear of having lost or eventually losing the meaning of our existence. This is what Tillich calls "the most important and most disturbing question in the quest for the courage to be." (10) He makes this claim because doubt and meaninglessness can undermine the courage by which we meet the other anxieties. If there is no meaning even in such courage, then courage itself is swallowed by nonbeing, and we are left in despair at the edge of the abyss. The question then is this: Is there a courage which can conquer even this despair?

Tillich insists that the answer is a courage which includes the presence of doubt and meaninglessness while acting over and against them. Just as anxiety continues in the triumph of courage over fate and death, and over guilt and condemnation, so despair continues to be present in the triumph of courage over doubt and meaninglessness. The liberation is from within and not outside the situation of despair, and I believe it is the most difficult of Tillich's explanations to grasp. What he describes is so counterintuitive to the existential feeling of despair, only Herculean courage can rise above the despair while also experiencing it.

As we have previously shown, it takes doubt to doubt the triumph of doubt, and no meaninglessness can exist without an implicit affirmation of the self that is experiencing the meaninglessness. "The negative lives from the positive it negates." [11] This strange liberation is what Tillich calls the "courage of despair," where even the acceptance of despair is in itself an act of faith and on the boundary line of the courage to be.

It is important to remember in this discussion that Tillich is addressing despair which is the result of existential anxiety, and not the despair occasioned by pathologies. The latter is the object of medical healing, while the former needs what he calls "priestly help" (for persons who still retain some freedom and options in deciding how they will interpret and act on their despair). One of those options is the courageous decision to continuing living with despair while disallowing it to either paralyze or to be the absolute measure of one's worth and value.

Tillich the Human Being

Until now, this chapter and the previous one have relied almost altogether on abstract concepts to describe Paul Tillich's theology of the human condition and its existential options. Long after I had written both chapters, and only shortly before this manuscript was handed over to the publisher, it occurred to me that my readers might welcome a concrete example of what I've been theoretically describing. The example I've selected is taken from Tillich's own life. Although it is a last-minute insertion, and something I've never recounted to anyone before, I have some confidence that Tillich would approve its inclusion.

Allow me, first, to put the example in context. When Tillich reached the mandatory retirement age at Union Theological Seminary, New York, he was invited to teach at Harvard Divinity. In 1962, while at Harvard, and at the age of 75, he accepted my invitation to preach a sermon and present four lectures at the Northaven Methodist Church in Dallas, Texas. The church was a newly-formed congregation on the growing north edge of the city. Following post-graduate studies at Union – which included studies with Tillich – and after a three-year internship on the staff of a large church, I had been appointed Northaven's pastor.

During the four days Tillich was our guest in Dallas, my wife, Nancy, and I, enjoyed a number of conversations with him both in our home and while we showed him various sites around the city. During one of our conversations, he quite casually mentioned – almost as an aside – that he had been suffering from a "deep depression." He gave no further explanation, and neither Nancy nor I felt that the disclosure was, in any way, offered in a confidential context, or that Tillich expected us to further explore the subject with him. In fact, immediately following the reference, he moved on quickly to other subjects in the conversation. Later, Nancy and I remarked to one another how unusual it was for someone to be so unguarded in volunteering an acknowledgment most people treat as intimately personal and private. It was not until a number of years thereafter that we found an explanation for Tillich's manner in a book by Rollo May, entitled, *Paulus*. [12]

Following Tillich's death in 1966, his widow, Hannah, urged Rollo May to write a biography of him. May had been one of Tillich's students at Union Theological Seminary in the thirties, and through the years, a deep bond of friendship had grown between them. He subtitled the book *Reminiscences of a Friendship*. In a chapter on "The Agony of Doubt," May wrote of Tillich:

> *True, he was often depressed. It was a general motif running through his life, expressed in his emphasis on physical miseries, in his feeling continually overworked, and in his constant worry about doing his work well enough. He sometimes impressed people as a man beset by life.* [13]

May further observed that there was something unpretentious and genuine in Tillich's manner of acknowledging his depression without allowing it to overwhelm him or the people to whom he mentioned it. He says of Tillich:

> *... his depressions never made the rest of us depressed. It is the <u>repressed</u> depression that communicates itself to those around a person. We are more apt to feel depressed by the perpetually smiling individual than the one who is honestly sad. If we admit our depression openly and freely, those around us get from it an experience of freedom rather than the depression itself. And this is how it was with Paulus.* [14]

As Nancy and I, through the years, have recalled the privilege of spending those few days with Tillich, our memory of them is the opposite of depressive. Rather, we experienced a human being who, without guile, allowed himself to enter fully into every relationship, every encounter, and every moment with intensity and openness. When we visited the Temple Immanuel Synagogue, he sat in silence for a long period of time, absorbing the magnificence of recently installed Marc Chagall-designed stain-glass windows. (The Synagogue's senior Rabbi, Levi Olan, attended all of Tillich's lectures.) As we drove by White Rock Lake, he asked if we could stop for him to walk out on the pier. Nancy and I waited in the car as he stood for a long time, looking out over the water, with his face turned into the sun and the wind blowing through his hair.

Tillich's genius for presence was especially apparent in his personal relationships. He entered into every human encounter, allowing himself to be completely grasped by the experience. Following each of his lectures, we invited the audience to submit written question to him. I read the questions aloud, and Tillich, without taking any notes, not only answered every aspect of a question, but also commented on other implications the question evoked. Afterward, we drove him to our home to relax on a long, redwood, screened-in porch at the back of the house, and to visit with members of the congregation we had invited. Each evening, the porch would be crowded with a different group of people sitting on the floor, while Tillich sat in a rocker with a glass of sherry, enthusiastically enjoying his interaction with everyone. It was obviously his favorite part of the evening.

I do not presume to know whether, during this time in Dallas, Tillich continued to be troubled by depression. And, it is important to point out that Rollo May, psychotherapist and close friend, observed that Tillich not only knew the existential anxiety which is the human condition of us all, he contended as well with some depression having psychological roots. [15] But during that extraordinary week, it was clear to all of us that Paul Tillich was a man who savored every relationship and every moment with a great exuberance for life

Even if he was depressed, he was also his own best example of "the courage to *be*," affirming the self "in spite of."

The God above God

For Tillich, the ultimate source of the courage to be is the "God above God." Absolute faith in this God is not the usual faith in the God of theism described in earlier chapters as a person-like being with whom one has a personal relationship. Rather, absolute faith is being grasped by the God above a theistic God in such a way as to make self-affirmation possible in the midst of nonbeing and its anxieties. It is the courage to take radical doubt about God into one's self and live meaningfully.

This is not a state of being which appears beside other states of mind. That is, it does not suddenly appear when you quit doubting or despairing. Instead, it is always in, with and under other states of mind. Only as you are experiencing the existential anxiety of your own death or emptiness or guilt can you take that anxiety into the courage to be. At such a moment – although still existentially present – death, emptiness or guilt is overcome, as the utter absurdity of human existence is resoundingly swallowed up in "nevertheless!" "The courage to be is rooted in the God who appears when God has disappeared in the anxiety of doubt." (16)

This understanding of a "God above God," while bringing depth psychology and the Christian faith into a creative mosaic, is not a recently invented way of thinking about God. Historically, for Christians, faith in this God and the courage to be, are centered in Jesus' crucifixion/resurrection. From the abyss of God's absence, in the very jaws of the absurd, the author of Luke has Jesus cry, "My God, my God, why hast thou forsaken me?" And this is followed by the cry, "Father, into thy hands I commit my spirit." At that moment the power of death is vanquished and the Resurrection – described later by the early church in cosmic, mythic terms – is implied. (17)

In his *Systematic Theology*, Tillich argues that the Cross and the Resurrection cannot be separated; they are interdependent. "The Cross of the Christ is the Cross of the one who has conquered the death of existential estrangement." (18) This means that Cross and Resurrection both happened within existence. But the difference is that while the Cross took place in "the full light of historical observation, the stories of the Resurrection spread a veil of deep mystery over the event." (19)

For the disciples, what the Resurrection overcame was their sense that Jesus was no longer with them. What the Resurrection meant to them was not his bodily return, but his spiritual presence. This event happened to some of his followers "in the hours of his execution; then to many others, then to Paul; then to all those who in every period experience his living presence here and now." [20] Thus, for Christians, the saving work of Jesus as the Christ was his total participation in our existential estrangement and his victory over that estrangement through trust in the "God above God." To be in Jesus Christ is to join him in that victory. Put poetically, it is, in death, to place one's self in the "arms" of the Mystery that transcends being and nonbeing.

Liturgical References to God

The church has always struggled with the language by which we refer to God – especially in liturgy and prayer. On the cross, Jesus' own prayerful cry is not in language that refers to the "God above God," or to "the ground of being." [21] Rather, it is a language which endows the Mystery with the paternal, "Father." Since we can come no closer to the divine presence than through personal relationships with others, then it stands to reason that devotional references to the "God above God" would use personal nouns and pronouns.

The integrity of such usage, however, is in meanings that are symbolic and not literal. "Father," like other metaphors for the transcendent and eternal, points beyond a person-like being to the Alpha and Omega source of all being. Just as the language of love will always be the language of poetry and song, so will the language of liturgy and prayer. Devotion is a genre beyond the rational, confounding the empirical; it belongs to the lyrical, the mythological and the paradoxical.

Toward the end of *The Courage to Be*, Tillich the theologian speaks as Tillich the pastor. He refers to the paradox that is inevitably present in every divine-human encounter – a paradox upon which both the early Christianity of the New Testament and a Christianity come-of-age depend. At any time in history, Tillich concludes:

They are aware that if God encounters man God is neither object nor subject and is therefore above the scheme into which theism has forced him. They are aware that personalism with respect to God is balanced by a transpersonal presence of the divine....They are aware of the paradoxical character of every prayer, of speaking to somebody to whom you cannot speak because he is not "somebody," of asking somebody of whom you cannot ask anything because he gives or gives not before you ask, of saying "thou" to somebody who is nearer to the I than the I is to itself. Each of these paradoxes drives the religious consciousness toward a God above the God of theism. (22)

This paradoxical character of worship makes it possible for the most mature of Christians to consciously use personal references for the divine, knowing that such language is symbolic, and that it points beyond itself to a Mystery about which we can only sing, mythologize and tell marvelous stories.

Tillich's concluding vision for the church is as follows:

... a church which raises itself in its message and its devotion to the God above the God of theism without sacrificing its concrete symbols can mediate a courage which takes doubt and meaninglessness into itself. It is the Church under the Cross which alone can do this, the Church which preaches the Crucified who cried to God who remained his God after the God of confidence had left him in the darkness of doubt and meaninglessness. To be as a part in such a church is to receive a courage to be in which one cannot lose one's self and in which one receives one's world. (23)

Let us turn then to the question of this church's future in the coming decades of a new millennium.

Notes and References

1. Paul Tillich, *The Courage To Be*, New Haven, Conn., 1952, p. 32

2. *The Complete Works of Fredrich Nietche*, ed, Oscar Levy (London, T.N. Foulis, 1911), Vol. IV, trans. Thomas Common, 73, sec. 4

3. Quoted in the Washington Post, March 24, 2004, as an excerpt appearing in the May issue of Men's Journal, and taken from his forthcoming book, *Why Courage Matters*.

4. Washington Post Magazine, August, 22, 2004, Gene Weingarten, "Fear Itself," p. 40. I use this example of Israeli courage with some ambivalence, acutely aware that there are numerous examples of Palestinian courage I could have chosen. The tragic, self-defeating violence of the Israeli/Palestinian conflict has occasioned countless acts of life-affirming courage on both sides.

5. On November 2, 2003, the Washington Post reported a survey on the afterlife. 76 percent of the persons answering the questionnaire indicated a belief in Heaven, and nearly two-thirds of them expect to go there. About one-fifth of all respondents said they believe in reincarnation, and one-third think it's possible to talk with the dead.

6. Op. Cit., Paul Tillich, p. 170

7. Ibid., p.164

8. *The Shaking of the Foundations*, New York: Charles Scribner's Sons, 1948), p.102

9. Ibid., p. 162

10. Op. Cit., Paul Tillich, p. 174

11. Ibid., p.176

12. Harper & Row, New York, Evanston, San Francisco, London, 1973.

13. Ibid., p. 77

14. Ibid., p. 77

15. Ibid., pp. 77-85

16. Ibid., p. 190

17. A biblical literalist will have a hard time here, especially with the different versions reported in the synoptic gospels. Matthew and Mark present Jesus' final words as a bitter cry of doubt and defeat, while Luke insists on a final cry of trust and surrender. Which version is true? Actually, scholars of the Jesus Seminar find both versions to be taken from a pre-Markan passion narrative: "The Tale of the Vindicated Sufferer." In this story, the hero reacts characteristically to suffering, expressing his frustration (as in Matthew and Mark) and expressing his trust (as in Luke). This narrative is the template for all the passion stories of the Gospels – regardless of their variations. Their focus is not on the question, "What really happened?" Their real quest is, "What does it mean?" "Were we right to put our trust in him?" While each Gospel interprets the meaning of Jesus' suffering and death with different emphases on the heroic, the redemptive or the revelatory, there is a resounding "Yes" in all of them to the vindication of their trust in God. For further treatment of this subject, see Arthur J. Dewey's "Can We Let Jesus Die," p.p.135-159, and Stephen J. Patterson's "Consider Yourself Dead," p.p.161-186 in *The Once & Future Faith,* Polebridge Press, Willamette University, Salem Oregon, 2001

18. *Systematic Theology, Vol II*, The University of Chicago Press, Chicago, Illinois, 1957, p 153

19. Ibid., p. 153

20. Ibid., p. 157

21. Tillich, himself, advised against using "the ground of being" devo-

tionally.

22. Ibid., p. 187

23. Ibid., p. 188

Chapter VIII: Tomorrow's Christendom

The Future of Post-Theistic Christianity

As the reader is doubtlessly aware, the come-of-age Christianity which I have been describing is not the Christianity ordinarily associated with most churches. In fact, it is dwarfed considerably by a conservative version of Christianity expanding almost exponentially around the world, and giving every evidence of becoming a dominant force in a variety of cultures. This chapter considers the wide-spread reach of such religion, suggests criteria for evaluating it, and tentatively projects the future for a more mature and radical version of the Christian faith.

Christianity In The United States

The prevailing theology in American churches today, both conservative and main-line, is the theism described in earlier chapters. It is the concept of God as a personalized, unseen presence who protects, guides, and sometimes intervenes in the lives of believers. This being is directly accessible and intimately involved with persons.

In addition, the more conservative churches emphasize the blood-sacrifice of Jesus on the cross, believing literally that a ransom was required by some unseen power, and that this ransom assuages for our sins. By way of the crucifixion, Jesus "paid the price" and "died for us." They hold that because of his death, we are redeemed and assured of eternal life. Accepting Christ as "personal Lord and Savior" is, for them, an exclusionary event, and all other religions are considered futile and false. Persons outside of Christ are believed to be condemned to an eternal punishment. Such beliefs usually motivate conservative Christians to hold conservative ethical positions, and to be aggressively evangelistic toward others.

In the last century, the Dr. Carl F. H. Henry, along with evangelist Billy Graham, was one of conservative Christianity's most influential spokesmen. He was founder and editor of "Christianity Today" – a periodical with a large audience of clergy and lay readers in the conservative community. Upon his death in December of 2003, the Washington Post reported in an obituary article the following account of his first meeting with the renowned Protestant theologian, Karl Barth:

> *Identifying himself as editor of Christianity Today, Dr. Henry found his question preempted by Barth.*
>
> *"Did you say Christianity Today or Christianity Yesterday?" asked Barth.*
>
> *"Yesterday, today and forever," Dr. Henry replied.* [1]

Henry enjoyed telling this story not only because it highlighted his rejoinder to Barth, but also because it demonstrated his belief in the unconditional, unchanging absolutism of conservative Christianity.

While the conservative theism described above is where many members of mainline denominations would also locate themselves today, a majority of persons in those churches hold less rigid, more progressive points of view. By "mainline denominations," I am referring primarily to the United Methodist Church, the Episcopal Church, the Presbyterian Church (U.S.A.), the Evangelical Lutheran Church in America, the American Baptist Church, and the United Church of Christ. Most members of these churches take the Bible seriously without taking it literally, holding it to be "The Word of God" rather than the "words of God." The doctrinal positions of these churches, while biblically and historically grounded, are not stiff orthodoxies authoritatively enforced, and among most of their constituents there is a high tolerance for diversity in interpretations. At the same time, each of these denominations has undergone differing degrees of trauma and schism over such issues as the ordination of women, the ordination of homosexuals, and the marriage of gays and lesbians

– issues vehemently opposed by most conservative churches.

The theistic concept of God, which is the compelling, common feature of Protestant Christians in America today, is also the dominant view of Roman Catholics. Though some, especially in the United States, are questioning the church's rigid sanctions against birth control, the marriage of priests, and the ordination of women, theism continues to be the prevailing theology of laity and clergy.

While no analogy is perfect, and must always allow for exceptions, the parent/child analogy discussed early is particularly applicable to the gradations of theological maturity one finds in American churches. Conservative congregations have much in common with needy and dependent children who must be cared for and protected. Such persons are often overwhelmed by life, and require the assurance that they are safe, favored and secure in relation to an authority from beyond themselves. For them, God is in the role of "parent" to their "child."

Mainline churches have congregations closer to the adolescent paradigm, requiring guidance, a certain amount of counsel, and occasional direction. Like teenagers, they have outgrown a number of dependencies, and while experimenting with different ways of venturing into the world, need reassurances and tutoring. For them, God is in the role of "parent" to their "adolescent."

And, of course, in both conservative and mainline congregations – including Roman Catholics – exceptional persons can be found who are in the process of "giving up childish ways," and are rethinking the theological milieu in which they have been nurtured. For a variety of reasons, some of these persons are remaining uneasily in their original congregations and some are changing to more progressive churches. But on the whole, most of them are giving up on the institutional church entirely. They leave lamenting the loss of a community where they can question, search and struggle with new ways of being faithful Christians in a time of precipitous change and challenge. I would hope that in the pages of this book, such persons might find some reason to believe that they are not alone, and that rather than having outgrown Christianity, they have been growing toward a more mature awareness of what it means to be Christian in a post-theistic world.

What does the future hold for such a faith come-of-age?

Trends and the Future

It is well known that mainline denominations are losing members at an alarming rate. What may be less well known is that this is not a new phenomenon. Since the 1920s, most of the major Protestant denominations have been experiencing a four or five percent loss in each decade, with one exception – the late 1950s and the early 60s. The baby-boom of the post World War II years brought a dramatic upsurge to church memberships. But by the late 60s, net gains had become net losses, and the pattern of membership decline became as characteristic of future decades as it was of previous ones.

In fact, at the time of the postwar revival, there was considerable debate about just how serious these new members really were. The mass recruitment of suburbanites caused at least one United Methodist Bishop, John Wesley Lord, to suggest that many in the influx "had been starched and ironed before they were washed." Whether these years are really the shining benchmark against which the mainline churches should measure themselves is at least a point of view subject to some dispute.

By the late 1980s, Dr. William R. Hutchinson, Charles Warren Professor of History of Religion in America at the Harvard Divinity School was predicting continued membership decline. He forecast: "The mainline churches (*old-line* as some have suggested is probably the better term), while they won't pass away, will predictably continue to experience losses in 'market share' within the American religious economy." Those losses have continued as a pattern for each of the remaining decades of the last century and into the new millennium.

In the meantime, conservative churches have been growing almost exponentially. Since the Scopes trial, they have been booming at a rate roughly three times that of mainline churches. For a while, each of these new churches with an average attendance every weekend of 2,000 worshipers or more was referred to as a "megachurch." The United States presently has 840 megachurches, according to church growth consultant John N. Vaughn. [2] Some of them have grown so large, with average attendances of ten, fifteen, twenty thousand, that Texas-based church consultant Bill Easum has created a new category: the gigachurch. These churches are largely independent, evangelical, and of a decisively conservative theological persuasion.

This expansion has not been strictly a Protestant phenomenon. Thirty years ago, about 90 percent of Latinos in the United States were Roman Catholic. Today that number is about 70 percent, and it remains steady only because of high birth rates and new immigrants filling pews. According to Notre Dame's Center for the Study of Latino Religion, 15 percent of first-generation Latino immigrants to the United States are Protestant. By the third generation, that number climbs to 29 percent. Literally thousands are leaving behind the ritual and perceived formality of the Roman Catholic Church for the "personal experiences" and more demonstrative worship services of charismatic churches. [3]

From every indication in both Protestant and Roman Catholic religion, these trends will continue, and the "childish Christianity" which I described in the first chapter will continue to multiply and flourish.

The Global Scene

The spread of conservative Christianity in the United States is magnified at a global level. We are living at a time of remarkable religious expansion, and a book by Philip Jenkins, *The Next Christendom*, is a carefully documented account of this religious revolution and the coming of global Christianity. [4] While we were focusing on the movements of communism, feminism and environmentalism, (and more recently, terrorism), the explosive southward growth of Christianity in Africa, Asia and Latin America hardly registered on Western consciousness. We have only recently begun to sense the enormous religious, political and social implications of this development.

In Africa, during the decades of the last century, mainline churches gradually reduced the number of their missionaries. "Mission" was redefined as enabling the development of indigenous church leadership, while giving priority to the educational, agricultural and medical needs of people. The old caricature of the missionary as a soul winner with a Bible in one hand and a machete in the other, setting out to convert the natives, belongs more to the 19th century than to the 20th and 21st.

However, during the time when the number of Western missionaries declined, rather than a depletion of Christian congregations, there was a prolific expansion. A large number of African converts declared that God had given them a special mission, and that they were called to Africanize the Christianity which had come to them from American and European missionaries. New congregations described themselves as independent churches (AICs) and have mushroomed in a variety of locales from swollen cities to rural villages. Almost without exception, they are inclined toward religious fundamentalism. The Zionist churches have been among the fastest growing, springing from charismatic sects in late-nineteenth century North America, and known for their practice of faith-healing and speaking in tongues. According to Jenkins:

> *They adopted African customs, including polygamy, and in some cases, observed ritual taboos. They also resemble traditional native religions in their beliefs in exorcism, witchcraft, and possession. Some follow the customs of particular tribes, like the Zulus, and have to some extent become tribally based churches. Many groups practice distinctive pilgrimages and ritual calendars, which intertwine with older tribal cycles.* [5]

Today, around 75 percent of Ugandans are Christian, as are 90 percent of the people of Madagascar. [6] By the mid-century, there could be more active church members in Uganda than in the four or five largest European nations combined.

The Roman Catholic Church has shared in this dramatic growth, especially in former French and Belgian territories. In 1955, the church claimed 16 million Catholics in the whole of Africa. Today, there are 120 million, and the number continues to increase. [7]

Members of the Church of England in the British Isles are already massively outnumbered by those overseas, with Nigeria alone claiming 20 million baptized Anglicans. Jenkins estimates that by 2050, "the global total of Anglicans will be approaching 150 million, of whom only a small minority will be White Europeans." [8] Also, by that time, seven of the world's twenty-five most populous nations will be in Africa, and it will have become one of the world centers of Christianity.

In Latin America, there has been a similar explosion in church members. Pentecostalism has appealed particularly to the poor, such as Brazil's Blacks and Mexico's Mayan Indians. Although Blacks make up about half of Brazil's population, they represent only 2 percent of congressional representatives in the government and only 1.5 percent of Roman Catholic bishops and priests. Not surprisingly, they have been willing recruits for the evangelical Protestant sects that have flourished and elevated them to positions of responsibility and leadership. [9] Although the Roman Catholic Church is still the largest single religious presence on that continent, the church has seen millions of Latin American Catholics converting to Protestantism and Pentecostalism. In 1940, about a million Protestants were recorded in the whole of Latin America; today they make up around one-tenth of the entire population, some 50 million people. [10] In both Guatemala and Chile, the percentage is about one-quarter of the whole. [11]

Jenkins reports on one controversial example of the new Pentecostalism sweeping the continent. Although he cautions that the excesses of this case should not be used to generalize about all the rising churches, their amazing growth indicates a successful catering to a vast public hunger. His reference is to the Brazilian-based Universal Church of the Kingdom of God (IURD) founded in 1977 and reporting in the mid-1990s between 3 and 6 million members. It controls one of the largest television stations in Brazil, has its own political party, and owns a Rio de Janeiro football team. Exploiting its largely uneducated members, Jenkins finds:

> *The church sells special anointing oil for healing, and television viewers are encouraged to place glasses of water near the screen so they can be blessed by remote control. The IURD web site promises that "A miracle awaits you." Sometimes, this miracle takes the form of release from demonic powers. The church offers "strong prayer to destroy witchcraft, demon possession, bad luck, bad dreams, all spiritual problems" and promises that members will gain "prosperity and financial breakthrough." Believers are told, in effect, that prayer and giving operate on the same crass principle as secular investments: the more one gives to the church, the more material benefit can be expected in this life.* (12)

The Catholic response to the Pentecostal movement in Latin America and elsewhere has been the creation of a number of charismatic organizations of its own. One striking example is the El Shaddai movement in the Philippines. Although solidly Roman Catholic, it has amassed a huge following through its charismatic meetings designed to slow the Protestant penetration. Jenkins reports:

> *As in Pentecostal churches, there is a firm belief in God's direct intervention in everyday life, which different observers interpret in different ways. Some see this belief as a childlike faith in the divine presence, while for others, the new groups are teaching crass materialism. El Shaddai followers raise their passports to be blessed at services, to ensure that they will get the visas they need to work overseas. Many open umbrellas and turn them upside-down as a symbolic way of catching the rich material blessings they expect to receive from on high.*
>
> *... The movement probably has 7 million members across the Philippines,*

making them a potent political force, and it also has the nucleus for a tru-
ly global presence. (13)

Christian numbers have also been growing apace in societies around the Pacific Rim. Asian churches give evidence of standing at the beginning of a new Christian epoch. Although in 1951, the People's Republic of China expelled all foreign missionaries, an indigenous and autonomous Chinese Christianity soon came into being. The U. S. State Department suggests that today the Chinese Christian population may run as high as 100 million souls. This number of Christians is larger than the number in either France or Great Britain. (14)

One of the great Asian expansions of Christianity has been in Korea. In 1920, that country counted only about 300,000 Christians. The number has since risen to 10 to 12 million, around a quarter of the national population. Protestants outnumber Roman Catholics by about three to one, and as in Latin America, most of the growth has been Pentecostal. The Full Gospel Central Church in Seoul now has over half a million members, and is reported in the *Guinness Book of Records* as the world's largest single congregation. Some mainstream denominations have also succeeded remarkably as evidenced by The Kwang Lim Methodist Church with 150 members in 1971 and 85,000 by the end of the century. Presbyterians in South Korea outnumber their counterparts in the United States almost two to one. (15)

Of all the numerical expansions, none has been more dramatic than the growth of Pentecostalism. Sparked in Los Angeles in 1906 by the preaching of William J. Seymour in a sermon which included a strange babbling language, Pentecostalism today has between 250 and 500 million adherents. Most of those converts are in the developing nations such as Brazil, China, the Philippines and Nigeria. It is the fastest-growing Christian movement in the world. Thirty years ago, Pentecostals, or similar charismatic groups, represented 6 percent of all Christians; today that figure is 25 percent, according to the *World Christian Encyclopedia*. (16)

Phillip Jenkins asserts that by the year 2050 only one Christian in five will be a non-Latino white person and the center of gravity of the Christian world will have shifted firmly to the Southern hemispheres.

Christendom's Future

There is much to affirm in the dramatic expansion of the Christianity we have been describing. Just as the art of Western Christianity has portrayed Jesus as having a physical appearance not too unlike our own, so the religious art of the Southern hemispheres has reflected a Jesus whose physical features offer a far more cosmopolitan perspective. In the realm of biblical images, many of the New Testament's agricultural metaphors which have become remote for modern urban and suburban dwellers – separating wheat and chaff, grafting vines, new and old wineskins – retain great relevance and meaning for persons in developing countries. There has also been a rich enculturation of Western liturgies and practices using vernacular language and indigenous customs such as drumming, dancing and clapping. Perhaps the most important value of all in the globalization of Christendom has been the millions of marginalized people who have found great meaning in their identification with a Jesus who challenged the powerful and rich, while reaching out to the poor, the outcasts and the oppressed.

At the same time, it is important to identify the excesses of the Zionist in Africa, the IURD in Brazil, and the *El Shaddai* in the Philippines as reasons for concern, and to acknowledge that there are more than a few instances in the Southern churches where "Pentecostal" fervor is a thinly disguised continuation of pagan practices. In fact, some of the African independent churches have retained tribal traditions of polygamy, divination, animal sacrifices, initiation rites, circumcision, and the veneration of ancestors. [17] However, these examples are exceptions and not the rule.

Even so, the common denominator of almost all of the new churches is a conservative theism centered in the firm belief that God intervenes directly in everyday life. To quote one observer of Brazil's emerging churches: "Their main appeal is that they present a God that you can use...People today are looking for   solutions, not for eternity." This is not surprising when one reflects on the poverty and suffering associated with Third World populations. It is understandable that so many threats at once – AIDS and other diseases, hunger, exploitation, pollution, violence, alcohol and drug addiction – would cause people to respond to almost any religious promise of miraculous solutions. If God will extricate demonic spirits, cure a sick child, deliver a spouse from addiction, provide a job after months of unemployment – these are powerful incentives to join a church claiming to mediate divine intervention.

Also, such churches usually practice a conservative morality and ethics. The leadership and ordination of women is generally opposed, critical political and social issues are seldom addressed, and in some instances, the AIDS epidemic has been indirectly advanced by church's opposition to the use of condoms. As with conservative Christians in America today, most Third World Christians consider homosexuality a grievous sin. This particular issue surfaced rather dramatically at the 1998 Lambeth Conference of the world's Anglican bishops who were considering an affirmative statement on homosexuality. The statement was roundly defeated due to the votes of Asian and particularly African bishops, causing Bishop John Spong of Newark to exclaim that the African bishops had "moved out of animism into a very superstitious kind of Christianity." [18]

A conservative social ethic has not always dominated Southern Roman Catholic churches. From 1958-1963, during the reign of Pope John XXIII and following the Second Vatican Council of 1963-65, liberation theology spread like wild fire through a number of developing Latin American nations. In the last quarter of the twentieth century, churches in many developing countries took up the plight of the poor and joined in organizing opposition to repressive regimes. A multiplicity of base communities came into being as seeds of a new society emerging from the shell of the old, and by the late 1970's, 80,000 such communities were reported in Brazil alone. However, with the election of John Paul II in 1978, a conservative pope silenced liberation theologians, made new episcopal appointments over the next twenty years, and eventually brought the church into a much more conservative line – a line presently sanctioned by Pope Benedict XVI. The base communities eventually withered, and over time, the plight of the urban poor was taken up by a Pentecostalism promising miracles and other tangible rewards.

Occasional Exceptions

Despite the rightward shift of churches in Latin America, there remain vestiges of the liberation movement in scattered places. In 1997, I received a leave of absence from my congregation for the purpose of, among other things, visiting base communities in Mexico. My wife and I lived for ten days in a retreat center outside of Cuernavaca. The center was sponsored by the Benedictine Sisters of Our Lady of Guadalupe – one of the most effective religious orders working with the poor in Mexico. The sisters are not cloistered and wear no habits. With the exception of a few who maintain the retreat center, the others live in small compounds throughout the countryside. Each morning they catch local buses that take them further into rural areas. Their days are spent teaching children, training homemakers in basic nutrition and health care, and conducting Bible study. They also lead daily services of praise, prayer and singing. All of this sounds relatively benign. But once the people discover Jesus' advocacy for the poor, and the worth and value that they are to God, a life-changing energy appears. They begin assuming responsibility for their own destiny, insisting on dignity and justice for themselves and for their children.

At the retreat center, our schedule included morning lectures on Mexican history and studies in Liberation Theology. In the afternoons, we visited base communities in rural areas nearby, including the village of Nopalera. Arriving at this village, we found the people still celebrating the success of a 300 strong delegation which had gone to the governor's office in the state of Morales to insist on water and electricity for Nopalera. Previously, all the utilities of the village had been discontinued because of a small number of delinquent accounts. The delegation's show of unity and purpose succeeded, and their success was a prime example of a community empowered by the Gospel.

In 2001, four years later, I found myself on a different continent, in a different developing country, and in another rural village of poverty and deprivation. I was in Muchinkike, Zimbabwe. It is typical of rural communities and urban centers throughout a country where unemployment, hunger, AIDS, and unmitigated suffering are so rife as to be almost beyond description. These conditions are due directly to decades of repression and the bankrupt policies of President Robert Mugabe, who South African Nobel peace laureate Desmond Tutu has referred to as "a cartoon figure of an archetypical African dictator." [19] The group I was with came with financial, technical and medical resources that could help the people help themselves. We were soon impressed with the village's eagerness to assume responsibility and take initiatives for addressing their situation, albeit the government's policies severely limited much of what they tried to do.

What struck me as the major difference between this African village and the one in Mexico was the role played by the church in the life of the people. In Nopalera, the Christian community was the focus of the village's vitality and self determination. In Muchinkike, and other population centers I visited in Zimbabwe, the churches were preoccupied with a fundamentalist theology and pietistic legalism which virtually ignored the social, political and economic crises all around them. Although I hasten to acknowledge that I became friends with several indigenous clergy who were literally risking their lives to oppose Mugabe's stranglehold on the nation, it was readily apparent that most of Christianity in Zimbabwe is typically the same conservative Christianity found throughout other developing nations in the Southern hemispheres. [20]

If history is any precedent, the new churches that have appeared as a result of the Southern expansion may eventually become less conservative. Movements over a period of time often become denominations – more organized, institutionally managed and educationally oriented. However, the resurgence of a more rigid conservatism in the Roman Catholic Church, and a dominant conservatism in the dramatically expanding independent churches, suggests the absence of any guarantee that time will eventually assure a more progressive Christianity. While I cannot presume that my brief experiences in Mexico and Zimbabwe are emblematic of religious trends in the countries or the continents where they occurred, there is a preponderance of evidence to support the prediction of Philip Jenkins when he says:

> *For the foreseeable future, the characteristic religious forms of Southern Christianity, enthusiastic and spontaneous, fundamentalist and supernatural-oriented, look massively different from those of the older centers in Europe and North America. This difference becomes critically important in light of current demographic trends. In the coming decades, the religious life characteristic of those regions may well become the Christian norm.* [21]

Christianity and Numbers

While the growth of conservative Christianity is an important trend at this time in history, its numerical success is not the final arbiter of its faithfulness. One of the most dramatic periods of church expansion was in the 4th Century, under the Roman Emperor, Constantine. His triumphant increase in church membership was, by and large, coerced and superficial. Today, the global ascendancy of fundamentalist, ultra-conservative Christianity is no more an assurance of its verity than would be the case if it were appearing among more liberal, progressive churches. The credibility of the Gospel has never been subject to "Gallop Polls for Jesus," and the validation of integrity and truth has never been guaranteed by majority opinion.

To be sure, there have been times in history when an authentic Christian witness has resulted in great expansion. One of the fruits of the first Pentecost Sunday was: "the Lord added to their number day by day" and Paul's missionary journeys through the Mediterranean world had enormous numerical impact. My own denomination sprang from the 18th century crowds that John Wesley preached to in open fields and at the entrances to mines. Time and again, faithfulness to the Gospel has added to the church's numbers.

But this increase was never automatic or assured. Unlike malignant cells, truth does not inexorably reproduce itself and spread. Sometimes the church's witness has been a minority opinion. Sometimes it has led to a loss in numbers. Sometimes it has stood alone.

The "faithful remnant" is a theme in both Old and New Testaments, and the numerical composition of that remnant, as defined by God, has usually been less than what most people expected. In the last century, there is probably no more striking example of vitality and integrity in smallness than that of the Confessing Church, the underground community of Christians refusing to allow the church to become a handmaid of the Third Reich. Their number was minuscule in comparison to the official, state Church of Germany. So was the size of the church before Constantine when Christians worshiped in the catacombs and risked being sent to the Coliseum or burned as human torches to light the revelries of Nero's garden. And, surely, Christ's own crucifixion by the multitudes in his day is our premier reminder of what faithfulness can lead to in any day – the "many" reduced to one.

While there may well be sound criteria for affirming the rapid spread of Christendom in the Southern hemispheres, this dramatic increase is not *ipso facto* proof that fidelity is found in numbers. There is only one sure promise that has nurtured and sustained the church: "For where two or three are gathered in my name, there am I in the midst of them."(Matthew 18:20) [22] Numbers can never be the sole criteria for defining faithful Christians.

"The body of Christ" Today

If my reader presently has no community of faith, I would hope this chapter might well provoke the question: "Where do I go and how do I become involved in such a Christian community today?" This question is inevitable if one takes seriously Dietrich Bonhoeffer's claim that Christ's "body" in the world will always occupy space and manifest itself as "life together." "Church" with a capital "C" can only be found in history as "church" with a lower case "c", and every Christian – no matter how "mature," "radical" or "committed" -- is an institutional Christian.

Since the church exists to show the "principalities and powers" of this world that they exist, "under God," to serve the cause of human dignity and justice, where does one find, today, expressions of that mission? After half a century of looking, I can only say: "in fragments." But then, of course, that's precisely what it means to be human, finite and imperfect. So I will speak of "fragments."

The institutional church, itself, for all its contradictions, is one of the more prominent of options. But one must look carefully here, lest contradictions so dominate a particular congregation, that its true purpose is overwhelmed and lost. The following components of an authentic community of faith are to be considered and inquired about.

Are there aspects of a church's worship which nurture one's sense of mystery and awe, without invoking supernatural interventions or resorting to magical incantations? Is prophetic judgment offered, followed by confession, proclamation and celebration of God's faithfulness and mercy? Is an opportunity provided for the community to show concern for each other as well as for the destitute and needy in the world? Are all of these components dramatized and symbolized in ways that prepare the congregation to return to the world exemplifying through their deeds that "Christ is risen!" because *they* are risen? (I Corinthians 15:12-19)

Regardless of a church's size, large or small, one should also determine the congregation's seriousness about biblical and theological reflection. Are adult classes or other opportunities offered where mature Christians can both learn and teach in contexts of genuine inquiry? Are provocative questions honored, including discussions of controversial subjects and 21st Century issues? Is there provision for persons to become familiar with modern biblical scholarship and the historical background of the scriptures? Serious study has always been and will always be integral to gatherings of Christians.

And, finally, no question about a congregation is more important than asking about its sense of mission: "Does it understand itself to exist for the purpose of renewing and revitalizing the world (as opposed to existing to perpetuate its own survival)?" If it is the former, a variety of mission ministries will almost surely engage the congregation. Some ministries may take the form of shelters and soup kitchens, or Volunteers in Mission and Appalachian Service Projects – all direct expressions of the church's caring for persons in their basic needs. Other ministries may be semi-church related, as in Habitat for Humanity and the Industrial Areas Foundation, while some are in the form or advocacy for justice and humanitarian concerns for the environment, peace, human rights, and other social issues.

Beyond the institutional church, are organizations like the Peace Corps and AmeriCorps, sponsored by the government, while many other organizations, now independent and self-supporting, were originally nurtured in the cradles of religious communities. One illustration of the latter is The Institute of Cultural Affairs, whose origin was in the Ecumenical Institute and its transformation of an inner city on the west side of Chicago. Today, the ICA is enabling peoples around the world to define and shape their futures, and is, in every sense, an expression of the church in mission. By caring for the basic needs of human beings, what all these ministries have in common is the power of their examples; they are demonstration projects saying: "Come on world, you can do the same."

A book by Hal Taussig entitled, *A New Spiritual Home*, reports a fledging appearance of what he calls "grassroots, progressive Christianity." It is drawn from a national research study of small, proliferating Christian communities which emphasize creative worship, feminism, gay-friendliness, progressive social issues, and a high tolerance toward other religions. Of course, it remains to be seen whether this phenomenon will gain enough traction to become a viable alternative to mainline denominations, but it is at least a welcome option for those today who find themselves outside of denominational churches. (Polebridge Press, Santa Rosa, California)

This chapter must not conclude without mentioning one other option: Mature Christians who, for whatever reason, find themselves removed from any ecclesiastical options, still have left their own initiative. By gathering like-minded persons at a certain time and in a certain place, they can act out together the rudimentary components of a Christian congregation: worship, study and mission. Whether meeting in the out-of-doors, a store front, or a home, such simple expressions of community have an honored place in the church's history of faithful configurations. That history began almost two thousand years ago, underground, in the catacombs of Rome.

One of the most radical books I ever read was *The Layman in Christian History*. In early chapters, different church historians write about what the church was like before it had an ordained clergy. There are accounts of the disciplines by which lay persons prepared themselves for the sacrament of baptizing other laity, and the prerogative of hearing the confession of a brother or sister in Christ, and therein offering forgiveness. Eventually, clergy where ordained by the laying on of hands by the laity, and when bishops were chosen, they were elected by the laity. But even at that time, and later, marriage rituals were administered by the lay contracting parties, laity served as the front line of the church's pedago-gy, and laity served as the church's chief arm for ministering to the sick and needy. (Edited by Stephen Charles Neill and Hans-Ruedi Weber, Westminster, 1964)

> *So, even if you're feeling all alone -- lay or clergy -- remember, "No excuses." The living church is in your hands, along with a magnificent tradition on behalf of bold initiatives and creating "life together."*

Notes and References

1. Washington Post, December 11, 2003

2. Ibid., May 15, 2004, B9. Vaughn's study, "Church Growth Today," took the average weekend attendance based on data reported by denomina-tional offices and independent churches as of May 13, 2004. The study does not include Roman Catholic parishes.

3. Ibid., April 30, 2006, Sonya Geis, A3, "Latino Catholics Increasingly Drawn To Pentecostalism"

4. Oxford University Press, Oxford, New York, 2002

5. Ibid., pp 52-53

6. Ibid., p. 44

7. Ibid., p. 58

8. Ibid., p. 59

9. Ibid., p. 74-75

10. Ibid., p. 61

11. Ibid., p.61

12. Ibid., p. 65

13. Ibid., p.67

14. Ibid., p. 70

15. Ibid., p. 71

16. The Washington Post, Ibid.

17. Jenkins, Op. Cit., p 120

18. Ibid., p. 121

19. Robert Mugabe once was hailed as a symbol of the new Africa, and Zimbabwe was once the breadbasket of the continent. Today, after decades of mismanagement, exploitation, and the most flagrant abuse of human rights, Zimbabwe is reported by the World Health Organization as having the world's shortest life expectancy – 37 years for men and 34 for women. It also has the greatest percentage of orphans (about 25%, says UNICEF) and the worst annual inflation rate (1,281 as of January, 2007). Mugabe last allowed an election in 2002, but "won" only after he had his leading opponent arrested for treason.

20. On November 4, 2006, the Associated Press reported that leaders of the Roman Catholic Bishops Conference, the Zimbabwe Council of Churches and Evangelical Fellowship were asking for forgiveness for failing their nation as Zimbabwe slid into what they called a "sense of national despair and loss of hope." The clerics said principles of peace, justice, forgiveness and honesty had degenerated and that even some church leaders "have been accomplices in some of the evils that have brought our nation to this condition." "Clearly, we did not do enough as churches to defend these values and raise an alarm at the appropriate time," they said. The churches resolved to foster free debate on such issues as the need for reforms in draconian security and media laws, freedom of expression and tolerance along with constitutional changes to protect human rights and curb powers of the government and President Robert Mugabe. (Washington Post, November 4, 2006)

21. Jenkins, Op. Cit., p. 78

22. Jesus Seminar scholars find rabbinic parallels to this verse, and believe that one of the reasons Matthew designated Jesus as its author was to show it as a standard feature of Judean piety. *The Five Gospels*, Translation and Commentary by: Robert W. Funk, Roy W. Hoover, and the Jesus Seminar, Harpers, San Francisco, 1997. p. 217

Conclusion

One of the great ironies of the church's history has been its tendency to enfold Jesus in sacred and immutable doctrines, while his own life was a protest against such absolutes. What is so distinctive about his resistance to temptations, both in the desert and throughout the New Testament story, are his refusals to deny his own finiteness, and his rejection of any pretense to being a demigod. The final focus of this resistance was the crucifixion and his response to the taunt, "You who would destroy the temple and build it in three days, save yourself! If you are the Son of God, come down from the cross." (Matthew 27:40) [1] He just hung there, dying as a human being without recourse to superhuman powers or a cosmic intervention.

And yet, almost from that time forward, his followers interpreted the meaning of his life and death with systems and dogmas that soon became ultimate criteria for faith. Churches called on their elites to be "guardians of the faith," conducting heresy trials and excommunicating or expelling those who dared to question or oppose the prevailing "orthodoxy." How strange all of this would seem to one who taught no system and was unsystematic, anti-dogmatic and anti-authoritarian. "Neither will I tell you by what authority I do these things."

Karen Armstrong, noted for her exhaustive analysis of Christianity and other religions, makes an observation that is provocative enough to quote at length:

> It is interesting that Christianity has been so particularly concerned about the doctrinal formulations of ineffable truth. It is very difficult to find a single doctrinal definition in the teaching of Jesus, who, like the prophets, Lao Tzu and Buddha, seems remarkably insouciant about theology. We do not hear him pronouncing definitively on any of the dogmas that are now held to be essential to the faith: Original Sin, the

Incarnation, the Trinity, the Atonement. One suspects that Jesus might have been rather surprised by some of these theological ideas, since most of them evolved centuries after his death. St. Augustine's doctrine of Original Sin, St. Athanasius's formulation of the Incarnation, the Cappadocian Fathers' Trinitarian dogma, or St. Anselm's theology of the Atonement all seemed a good idea at the time. ...Just because they have once been very helpful to Christians in the past does not mean that we need to lug them around with us forever. All too often such doctrines can become a mental fetter, impeding us from enlightenment. Like Augustine, Athanasius and Anselm, we should perhaps create our own ways of speaking about Christianity. [2]

In a world come-of-age, the parent/child analogy has been this author's way of trying to speak about a Christianity that distinguishes between a *childish* faith of helplessness and dependency and a *childlike* faith of maturity and humility. At the same time, humility itself requires the admission that none of us knows for sure who really qualifies for the biblical concept of a "faithful remnant." My hunch is that such qualification has less to do with right belief and more to do with acts and deeds. And in the end, above all else, it will depend on a grace and mercy beyond our selves.

So I cannot presume that the interpretations I have offered in these pages, or the theologians I have relied upon, are without error or distortion. While it has been my intention to be both faithful and creative in discussing certain traditions of the Christian faith, I have no doubt that what I've written is as limited and as historically conditioned as the theological positions I have attempted to contemporize. But this is the way of theology, and surely there will be other persons offering correctives and critiques of my interpretations, as well as persons offering more original and innovative contributions of their own. Thus we keep alive what Tillich called "The Protestant Principle" of maintaining the vitality of the church through the duality of tradition and reformation.

My quarrel with conservatives is not that their truth is necessarily inferior to mine. While I am earnestly convinced of the propositions I've set forth, I am certain that both our "truths" are limited and finite, and that the most either of us can hope for is a theological approximation of what it means to say: "Jesus Christ is Lord." We will always have this treasure in "earthen vessels."

What I find most regrettable about my conservative friends is their desperate willingness to trade truth for certainty. Truth always comes indirectly, paradoxically, and is never "obvious." Therefore, it is inherently subject to interpretation and a leap of faith. Conservatives fail to see that their definition of truth as "revealed certainty" is, itself, interpretation and a leap of faith. Their presumed absolutes and dogmas are but a camouflage for the unsettling discovery that what they seek is not self evident. When the existential anxiety of living with uncertainty is more than one can bear, then "faith" becomes a desperate clinging to the authoritarian and immutable.

But this is not the faith set forth in the 11th Chapter of Hebrews, where faith is taking a chance on the unproven, the not yet come to pass, "...the assurance of things hoped for, the conviction of things not seen." [3] And it is never knowing for sure what lies ahead: "All of these died in faith without having received the promises, ..." [4] Such faith takes courage. Not courage born of bravado, but courage that has its origin and aim in God. To choose such courage is to decide to be, not *childish*, but *childlike*, trusting that the God beyond God is for you and not against you. It is to bet your life and death, to gamble human destiny itself on an eternal reality made manifest in human relationships, and made most manifest in the extraordinarily human life of Jesus.

If, in my final moments of consciousness before death, or even after death – whatever "after death" turns out to be – it is proven conclusively to me that the theists were right after all, and that God exists as a person-like, super being, requiring childish dependency and uncritical acceptance of certain absolutes – I will have no regrets about the way I've lived or what I've written here. As inadequate and imperfect as my life and this little book most surely are, I would rather have lived in awe of the Mystery I've encountered daily, and by the gamble I have made on *love*. If that Mystery and *love* are not the *sine qua non* of Jesus' life and teachings – I'm without a clue!

I can think of nothing more wondrous than loving and being loved, and nothing more nihilistic or tragic than living as though love doesn't matter. It matters! It matters to each of us. Ultimately, it *is* our life. And, at the existential level of our being, it is self-authenticating, lived only as a gift.

I conclude with a Hasidic story that sums up preceding chapters, and implies the rationale for all I've written.

> *Once there was a rabbi who disappeared every Shabat Eve "to commune with God in the forest," so his congregation thought. One Sabbath night they deputed one of their cantors to follow the rabbi and observe the holy encounter. Deeper and deeper into the woods the rabbi went until he came to the small cottage of an old Gentile woman, sick to death and crippled into a painful posture. Once there, the rabbi cooked for her and carried her firewood and swept her floor.*
>
> *Then when the chores were finished, he returned immediately to his little house next to the synagogue. Back in the village the people demanded of the one they'd sent to follow him. "Did our rabbi go to heaven as we thought?" "Oh, no," the cantor answered after a thoughtful pause, "our rabbi went much, much higher than that."*

Notes and References

1. Jesus Seminar scholars think that Jesus may have made some remark about the destruction and building of the temple, but they doubt he tied that prediction to a three-day interval. The remainder of the taunt, "If you're God's son, come down from the cross," is actually Matthew's language. He is here advancing a claim on Jesus' behalf rather than reporting something Jesus said.

2. Karen Armstrong, *The Once and Future Faith*, Polebridge Press, Santa Rosa California, 2001, p. 26-27

3. *NRSV*, verse 1

4. Ibid., verse 13

About the Author

William A. Holmes is Minister *Emeritus* of United Methodism's National Church in Washington, D.C., Metropolitan Memorial. After 24 years as the Church's Senior Minister, he retired in 1998.

Holmes experience includes work as an author, lecturer, and television host. His writing includes, *Tomorrow's Church, A Cosmopolitan Community*, Abingdon Press, 1968, *Careers for Clergy*, Chapter I, "The Pastor," Consortium Press, 1976; and *Nonviolence: Origins and Outcomes*, Chapter VIII, 2003. He has had articles in the *Harvard Divinity Bulletin* and *The Progressive Christian*, and sermons published in *A Man Named John F. Kennedy*, Paulist Press; 1964,"The Christian Century;" and *Sermons On Suicide*, Westminster Press, 1989. He was also the host for the weekly television program, "Perspective," on WDVM, CBS, Washington, D.C.

Excerpts from his 1963 sermon on the assassination of John F. Kennedy, preached at Dallas' Northaven United Methodist Church, were carried on the "CBS Walter Cronkite Evening News." He has been a preacher for The Protestant Hour, a preacher and lecturer for "Ministers Week" and other keynote events at Perkins School of Theology, Boston University School of Theology, Duke Divinity School, Wesley Theological Seminary, and Candler School of Theology at Emory. He also served as a preacher for United Methodist Annual Conferences in Western Pennsylvania, New Jersey, North Dakota, North Carolina and Arkansas; and as the lecturer for Pastors' Schools in 16 states.

While in Washington, D.C., Holmes served on the Governing Board of the National Council of Churches, chaired the Task Force on Homosexuality for the Baltimore-Washington Conference, founded the Lawyer's Guild, and served as Chairman of the Ethics Advisory Committee and trustee of Sibley Memorial Hospital.

He is married to Nancy Murray; they have two grown sons, Will and Chris, six grandchildren, and make their home in Maryland.

LaVergne, TN USA
05 December 2010
207477LV00004B/223/P